Praise for the Weird & Wacky Holiday Marketing Guide through the years . . .

"Ginger Marks' "2017 Weird & Wacky Holiday Marketing Guide" is a compendium of ideas to market your product, tying it to state, national and international celebrations of every conceivable kind. The research done for this book is mind-boggling. The holidays are organized by month, and list month-long, week-long and daily holidays. Appendix A provides a huge number of ready-made materials that you can use for blog posts, flyers, press releases, etc. If you're looking to jump-start your marketing, you must get this book. Highly recommended." — **A Writer** (2017 Edition)

"As someone who's taught "Marketing Your Biz on a Shoestring for years," I always note the value of fun/crazy/unusual holidays for adding to your marketing options. Ginger's put together a great guide that gives you EVERYTHING: serious holidays, regularly scheduled holidays and just for fun stuff. (Ever heard of "Poetry at Work Day?" That's as I write this, on Jan. 10.)

Instead of spending hours surfing the 'Net for ideas (hours = $$$ folks) use this all-in-one idea sparker!" —**Bklyngal535** (2017 Edition)

"People love to buy. They especially love to buy when they have a reason. The *Holiday Marketing Guide* provides clever marketing strategies to increase sales every month of the year based on events and holidays. It's a brilliant guide for the savvy marketer." —**Daniel Hall,** Creator of Free Marketing Tutorials at DanielHallPresents.com (2016 Edition)

"Ginger Marks has put together a fantastic resource! If you are looking for outside of the box ideas for marketing as well as for celebrating, you are going to love the Weird & Wacky Holiday Marketing Guide. As a former elementary school teacher, I wish I had had a copy of this incredible resource when I was teaching. The month-long and week-long holidays, listed throughout this guide, could create the foundation for exciting study units." —**D'vorah Lansky, M.Ed.** Best-Selling author of Book Marketing Made Easy, www.BookMarketingMadeEasy.com (2016 Edition)

"Another awesome read from Ginger packed with quick grab and go marketing ideas to expand your space in this world. Let's face it, in order to capture attention, there has to be a creative hook. What better way to align your marketing than with holiday's that offer a creative roll out. The ideas and positioning for each month are fun and creative with a unique flare. Highly recommend this book for those who are looking for the creative edge." —**Lauren E Miller,** Google's #1 Stress Relief Expert/International Best-Selling Author/Speaker/Trainer/Coach, www.LaurenEMiller.com (2016 Edition)

"So much info in one book! As a business owner, it's difficult to stand out. With Ginger's guidance you can set yourself apart from the crowd. It's well-written and easy to follow. Tons and tons of info and well worth it!" — **Patti Knoles, Virtual Graphic Arts Department** (2017 Edition)

"Great information, simply organized to assist in planning a marketing strategy that is fun and effective! Educational too." — **Debra Stoks,** Author, The Green Coat: What Love Looks Like (2017 Edition)

2018 *Weird & Wacky*
10th Edition

HOLIDAY MARKETING GUIDE

Your business marketing calendar of ideas

Ginger Marks

DocUmeant *Publishing*

244 5th Avenue
Suite G-200
NY, NY 10001
646-233-4366
www.DocUmeantPublishing.com

10th Edition, December 2017

Published by DocUmeant Publishing
244 5th Ave, Ste G–200
NY, NY 10001
646-233-4366

Editor Wendy VanHatten
VanHatten Writing Services
www.wendyvanhatten.com

Layout and Design Ginger Marks
DocUmeant Designs
www.DocUmeantDesigns.com

Library of Congress Control Number: 2017918998

ISBN: 978-1-9378-0187-8

Contents

Foreword

Events are one of the smartest prescriptions for slumping sales and for maintaining a healthy business. It's not enough anymore to merely have goods on the shelf and open the doors on time every day. We all need to reinvent our businesses to keep them thriving and healthy. And, that is just what this book helps you achieve.

This unique marketing book continues to win awards year after year and remains a #1 Best-Seller in the Business Marketing genre. Highly praised by marketing experts and now in its tenth edition, this book offers more fun and easy marketing ideas exclusively penned for the calendar year 2018. Now you can grow your business with strategies built around wacky holidays, observed throughout the world, for the entire 2018 calendar year. If you missed the premier 2009 issue or want to complete your collection, all previous and unique yearly editions are available at http://www.HolidayMarketingGuide.com.

As Weird & Wacky Holiday Marketing Guide is now read and used internationally I have included many International Independence Day listings and US State Fairs. In future editions, you will most likely find additional International holidays listed. However, for now, I thought I would get you used to seeing other countries represented with their respective Independence Day listings.

To take advantage of the information provided, pick a day and discover the unusual holidays celebrated on that date. Then, read the corresponding month's "Holiday Marketing Ideas" section to find a simple implementation or allow it to open your creative mind and think of some of your own.

Please note that the asterisk (*) in front of a holiday means a specific holiday is celebrated on that numerical date each year. For example, Christmas Day is December 25 no matter what day that falls on during the calendar week.

Here's another exceptional marketing idea for you I discovered when visiting BrownieLocks. com back in 2009, and which is now listed in the official Chase Calendar of Events which I cull from every year. Bonza Bottler Days™—the day is the same as the month it is in. That equates to: 1/1, 2/2, 3/3, etc. There is one in every month. There you have it; another extra fine excuse for an event to boost your notoriety and sales each and every month!

This is by no means a comprehensive edition. I have made all attempts to ensure the accuracy of the contents. If you encounter errors, or know of a holiday that needs to be included, please let me know so they can be addressed in future editions. But remember, if your suggested holiday addition is not listed in the official Chase Calendar of Events it is not eligible for inclusion.

Read on, have fun, initiate your own version of these holidays, and reap the benefit for your business.

Ginger Marks

P.S. I have included a new appendix section titled, "2018 Social Media Image Size Guide" to simplify your Weird & Wacky Holiday Marketing social media image creation. Look for it in the appendix section. You'll probably refer to it often enough to necessitate making a copy and keep handy.

P.S.S. The Weird & Wacky Holiday Marketing Companion Playbook. This tool is intended to help you to create, organize, and put the FUN back into your marketing plan. Each monthly calendar offers space for you to begin your planning and keep all your notes in one handy book. Since each year the physical calendar days rotate I have left the date numbers blank to enable you to make use of this Companion Playbook beginning today.

Companion Playbook for

Weird & Wacky Holiday Marketing Guide

Award Winning Author/Designer
GINGER MARKS

Annual Dates of Note

International Year of The Reef

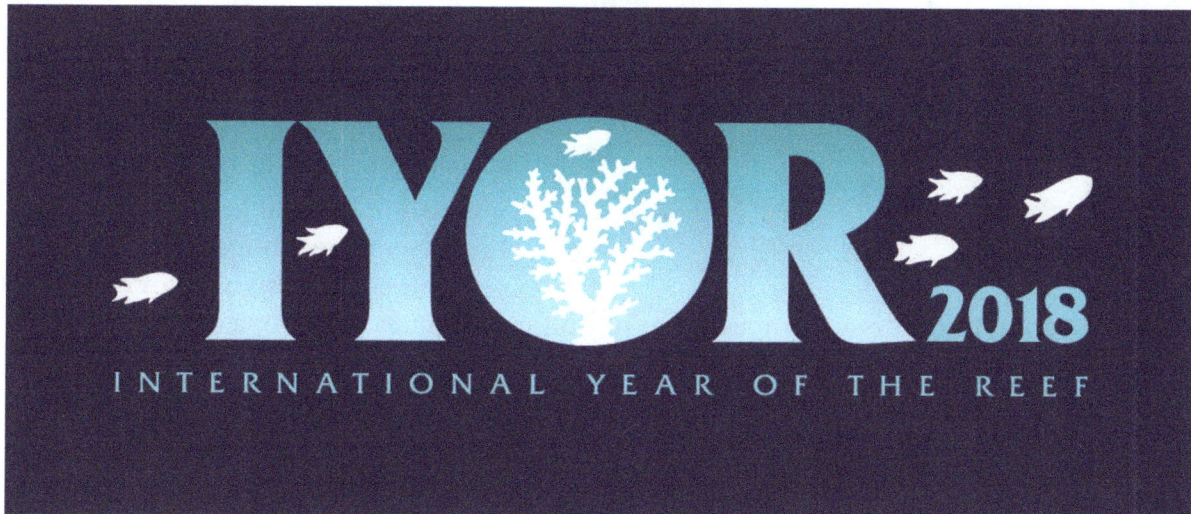

This is actually the third international year of the reef; previous observances were in 1997 and 2008. For 2018, the objectives are to strengthen awareness globally about the value of, and threats to, coral reefs and associated ecosystems and to promote partnerships among governments, the private sector, academia, and civil society on the management of coral reefs

Coral reefs —unique and diverse marine ecosystems — occur all over the world, in temperate and tropical waters. The greatest collections are in Southeast Asia and Australia. Australia's Great Barrier Reef is the largest reef system: about 215,000 square miles extending 1,430 miles along the eastern coast of the continental island. It was named a World Heritage Site in 1981. But it, as well as other reefs, is in danger of extinction. Some of the threat comes from pollution — the chemicals in sunscreen, for example, can damage reefs and their inhabitants. Overfishing is also a problem. The biggest danger is from warming water as a result of climate change. Warming water can trigger "coral bleaching", in which stressed coral expels the algae with which it has lived in balance. Without the energy the algae provide, the coral starves. The normally colorful coral turns a pale or white—looking 'bleached'. In areas hit by warming water and bleaching, up to fifty percent of the coral dies. Mass bleaching was not even noted prior to 1979.

It is with a sense of urgency, then, that the third international year of the reef was established in a global effort to research, recommend, and encourage awareness.

For more information visit International Coral Reef Initiative (ICRI) at www.icriforum.org.

European Year of Cultural Heritage

On April 27, 2017, the European Parliament adopted a proposal to designate 2018 as the European Year of Cultural Heritage. It is a year to explore Europe's rich and diverse cultural heritage — and to celebrate, understand, and protect its unique value.

There are currently 28 members of the EU. All members are expected to participate in this unique effort. 2018 will see activities and initiatives all around Europe to get people interested and involved in cultural heritage. At press time, events were not confirmed; please see the website to sign up for email alerts and to find out further news at European Year of Cultural Heritage (ec.europa.eu/culture/European-year-cultural-heritage-2018_en).

Chinese Year of the Dog[1]

Dog is the eleventh in the 12-year cycle of Chinese zodiac sign. The Years of the Dog include 1922, 1934, 1946, 1958, 1970, 1982, 1994, 2006, 2018, 2030, 2042 . . .

Dog is man's good friend who can understand the human's spirit and obey its master, whether he is wealthy or not. The Chinese regard it as an auspicious animal. If a dog happens to come to a house, it symbolizes the coming of fortune. The invincible God Erlang in Chinese legend used a loyal wolfhound to help him capture monsters.

People born in the Year of the Dog are usually independent, sincere, loyal, and decisive according to Chinese zodiac analysis. They are not afraid of difficulties in daily life. These shining characteristics make them have harmonious relationship with people around.

Strengths
Valiant, loyal, responsible, clever, courageous, lively

Weaknesses
Sensitive, conservative, stubborn, emotional

---

1 Travel China Guide. https://www.travelchinaguide.com/intro/social_customs/zodiac/dog.htm

Matches

Perfect: Rabbit

They are born to be a perfect match. Similar personality traits and common hobbies add much fun to their love relationship. They can understand each other and face difficulties with enough patience.

Avoid: Dragon, Sheep, Rooster

Different sense of worth may cause many conflicts in their daily life. Both of them are not willing to share inner true feelings. The lack of effective communication and trust won't bring a happy and relaxing marriage life.

Rooster's Personality by Blood Type

Blood Type O: They are brave, clever, honest, and optimistic. Outstanding work abilities and good tempers make them achieve a lot in early and middle lives.

Blood Type A: Helping others with all efforts is their biggest virtue. Extensive and stable interpersonal relationship can provide much necessary help to their career.

Blood Type B: They always try to achieve success by their own efforts. Honesty and optimism are their shining points.

Blood Type AB: With high self-control and prudence in their nature, they always obtain bosses' recognition in early and middle ages.

JANUARY

MONTH-LONG HOLIDAYS

Jan 6 – Feb 13 Carnival Season
Jan 7 – Feb 13 Germany: Munich Fasching Carnival

Be Kind to Food Servers Month, Book Blitz Month, Celebrate Life Month, Children Impacted by a Parent's Cancer Month, Clap4Health Month, Get Organized Month, International Child-Centered Divorce Month, International Creativity Month, International New Year's Resolutions Month for Business, National Clean Up Your Computer Month, National Glaucoma Awareness Month, National Hot Tea Month, National Mentoring Month, National Personal Self-Defense Awareness Month, National Poverty in America Awareness Month, National Radon Action Month, National Skating Month, National Slavery and Human Trafficking Prevention Month, National Stalking Awareness Month, National Volunteer Blood Donor Month, Oatmeal Month, Worldwide Rising Star Month

WEEK-LONG HOLIDAYS

Jan 1 – 3 Japanese Era New Year

Jan 1 – 7 Diet Resolution Week

Jan 2 – 5 Elvis Presley Birthday Celebration

Jan 2 – 8 Someday We'll Laugh about This Week

Jan 8 – 14 Dating and Life Coach Recognition Week

Jan 11-17 Cuckoo Dancing Week

Jan 12 – 14 Art Deco Weekend

Jan 14 – 20 Healthy Weight Week

Jan 15 – 19 Sugar Awareness Week

Jan 18 – 22 Creativation

Jan 18 – 25 Week of Christian Unity

Jan 20 – 21 Bald Eagle Appreciation Days

Jan 21 – 27 International Handwriting Analysis Week, National CRNA Week

Jan 22 – 26 Clean Out Your Inbox Week

Jan 28 – Feb 3 Catholic Schools Week

DAILY HOLIDAYS

1. Betsy Ross Birthday (1752), *Bonza Bottler Day™, Canada: Polar Bear Swim, *Copyright Revision Law Signed (1976), Cuba: Liberation Day and Anniversary of the Revolution, Czech–Slovak Divorce (1993; Anniversary of separation into two nations), *Ellis Island Opened Anniversary (1892), *Emancipation Proclamation (1863), *Euro Introduced (1999), *First Baby Boomer Born–Kathleen Casey Wilkens in Philadelphia, PA (1946), *Frankenstein Published (200th Anniversary), *Haiti: Independence Day, *Mummer's Parade, *National Environmental Policy Act (1970), *New Year's Day, *New Year's Dishonor List Day, Paul Revere Birthday (1735), Saint Basil's Day, Stock Exchange Holiday, *Z–Day

2. 55 MPH Speed Limit Day (1974), Haiti: Ancestor's Day, *Happy Mew Year for Cats Day, Japan: Kakizome, Switzerland: Berchtoldstag

3. *Alaska Admission Day, Congress Assembles, *Drinking Straw Day (1888), Earth at Perihelion, J.R.R. Tolkien Birthday Anniversary (1892), Memento Mori Day, Saint Genevieve Day

4. *Amnesty for Polygamists: Anniversary (125th Anniversary; 1893), *Dimpled Chad Day, *Elizabeth Ann Bayley–Seton Day, *Pop Music Chart Day, Sir Isaac Newton Birthday (1643), *Trivia Day, Utah: Admission Day (1896), *World Braille Day, World's Tallest Building Day

5. *Alvin Ailey (1931), *Five-Dollar-a-Day Minimum Wage Day (1914), National Bird Day, Twelfth Night

6. *Armenian Christmas, *Epiphany or Twelfth Day, Italy: La Befana, New Mexico: Admission Day (1912), Pan Am Circles Earth (1942), *Three Kings Day

7. *First Balloon Fight Across English Channel (1785), *Harlem Globetrotter's Day, *International Programmers' Day, Japan: Nanakusa and Usokae, Orthodox Christmas, Trans-Atlantic Phoning (1927)

8. Argyle Day, Asarrah B'Tevet, *Elvis Presley Birth (1935), National Clean Off Your Desk Day, *National Joygerm Day, National Thank God It's Monday! Day, Plough Monday, *Show and Tell Day at Work, *War on Poverty Day (1964)

9. *Aviation in America Day (1793), *Panama's Martyr Day, Poetry at Work Day

10. League of Nations Founding (1946)

11. Designated Hitter Day (1973), Learn Your Name in Morse Code Day, Morocco: Independence Day, Nepal: National Unity Day, US Surgeon General Declares Cigarettes Hazardous (1964)

12. *Haiti Earthquake Day (2010), National Hot Yea Day, *Women Denied Vote (1915)

13. Norway: Tyvendedagen, *Radio Broadcasting Day, Russia: Old New Year's Eve, Sweden: Saint Knut's Day

14. *Benedict Arnold Day, *Ratification Day, Switzerland: Meitlisunntig

15. Martin Luther King Birthday (1929), Molière Day, Quarterly Estimated Federal Income Tax Payers' Due Date (also Apr 16, Jun 15 and Sep 17, 2018)

16. *Appreciate a Dragon Day, *Civil Service Day, Japan: Haru-No-Yabuiri, *National Nothing Day, *Religious Freedom Day, Rid the World of Fad Diets and Gimmicks Day

17. *Al Capone Day, *Cable Car Day, *Ben Franklin Birthday (1706), *Judgment Day, Kid Inventors' Day, Mexico: Blessing of the Animals at the Cathedral, Saint Anthony's Day, Southern California Earthquake Day

18. Get to Know Your Customers Day (also April 19, July 19, and Oct 18, set aside to get to know your customers even better), *Louis and Clark Expedition Commissioned (1803), *Pooh Day

19. Arbor Day in Florida, *Confederate Heroes Day (Texas), Ethiopia: Timket, International Fetish Day, National Popcorn Day, Poe Day, *Tin Can Day

20. Brazil: San Sebastian's Day

21. Celebration of Life Day, First Concorde Flight, Kiwanis International: Anniversary, *National Hugging Day™, Stephen Foster Day

22. *Answer Your Cat's Questions Day, *Roe vs. Wade Day, *Saint Vincent Feast Day, Ukraine: Ukrainian Day

23. Bulgaria: Babin Den, *National Handwriting Day, National Pie Day, Snowplow Mailbox Hockey Day

24. *Belly Laugh Day, *Beer Can Day, *National Compliment Day

25. *A Room of One's Own Day, *Around the World in 72 Days Day, First Scheduled Transcontinental Flight, *Macintosh Computer Day (1984), Saint Dwynwen Day

26. Australia: Australia Day, Dental Drill Day, Dominican Republic: National Holiday, India: Republic Day, National Preschool Fitness Day

27. Apollo I: Spacecraft Fire (1967), Germany: Day of Remembrance for Victims of Nazism, Local Quilt Shop Day, *Mozart Day, National Geographic Society Day, National Seed Swap Day, *Thomas Crapper Day, United Nations: International Day of Commemoration in Memory of the Victims of the Holocaust, *Viet Nam Peace Day

28. *Challenger Space Shuttle Explosion (1986), Data Privacy Day, National Pediatrician Day, World Leprosy Day

29. Bubble Wrap Appreciation Day, *Curmudgeons Day, *Seeing Eye Dog Day

30. Blood Sunday, Inane Answering Message Day, Tet Offensive Begins: 50th Anniversary

31. First Social Security Check Issued Day, *Inspire Your Heart with Art Day, Nauru: National Holiday, Schubert Day, Tu B'Shvat

HOLIDAY MARKETING IDEAS FOR JANUARY

Clap4Health Month — This month's feature holiday reminds us that clapping is heathy! Once you start clapping you'll find it addictive. The suggestion I have for you is to host a 'Clap4Health Month' clap counter. Invite your friends to tick a 'clapper' to get counted every day. You might consider making it a contest by getting other businesses involved. The business could commit any amount they choose per clap. Have them host the clap counter on their website and whichever business gets the most 'claps' at the end of the month gives a donation by the sponsor to their favorite charity. Ask your sponsor to give one cent per

clap or one dollar, it's their choice. Why not be the sponsor yourself? Imagine all the businesses involved would host your logo as the sponsor on their website while promoting the contest. And, that would indeed be good for business!

At Clap4Health they will be happy to work with you. They offer:

- 20% of all proceeds goes to any organization that they choose and 80% goes back to Shape Up Us—Our mission "Building A Healthier Future for Children"

- And 100% of All Donations from Clapr4Health! will sponsor a teacher or school

- You can sign up for Clap4Health and join Shape Up Us

Even the media might pick up on this one. You'll find helpful information on how to get started here: https://clap4health.com/ and one of their flyers in the appendix.

Jan 1 Frankenstein Day—This being the 200th Anniversary of the first edition of this classic, this year is the ideal one to host your 'Frankenstein Day' event. You could have a drawing, photo op, or full-blown event. If you opt for the event, why not use an old Frankenstein movie poster, like I did for the bonus event 'Dracula Day' that I designed on the holidaymarketingguide.com website in 2017? Think about what Frankenstein symbolizes—things that frighten us, monsters in our closets, stuff that hampers our success, etc. Then, host an event that shares 'overcoming' ideas. You can do it all yourself, or ask coaches to participate, very easily with a little forethought and planning. Be sure to check the Sample Appendix for a premade poster you can adapt to your event.

Jan 12 Haiti Earthquake Day—It's time to shake things up! Exercise businesses and coaches have a readymade day to promote their business with this wonderful weird & wacky holiday. I can even envision cooks and authors of such as stirring things up to promote their books and businesses. What can you think of to stir up the marketing for your business?

Crabby Road   5-3

Looking on the bright side hurts my eyes.

©Hallmark Licensing, Inc.   Maxine

Jan 23 National Pie Day—Did you know there is a national holiday set aside to celebrate the biggest pie fight in history!? Have some fun and watch one now on YouTube here: https://youtu.be/aHY5SM0YFv0. Or what about your best 'pie-in-the-face' joke? Don't just think baking, have some real fun with this day. However, if you do want to bake, there's bake sales to fundraise for a charity, or even just to give to shut-ins or to your local shelter. If you are up to the task, let the media know what you are doing and get your business noticed.

Jan 29 Curmudgeons Day—Are you a grump or do you know a gump? This is your day. Celebrate today with Curmudgeons Day wishes for an especially grumpy day. Have a 'grump out' just for fun. See who can keep from laughing the longest as you make grumpy faces at each other. Or, have a grumpy photo contest. There are a few grumpy ways to spend your Curmudgeons day.

FEBRUARY

MONTH-LONG HOLIDAYS

Feb 14 – Mar 31 Lent
Feb 19 – Mar 30 Orthodox Lent

AMD/Low Vision Awareness Month, *American Heart Month, Bake for Family Fun Month, Declutter for a Cause Month, Feline Fix by Five Month, Library Lovers Month, Marfan Syndrome Awareness Month, National African American History Month, National Bird-Feeding Month, National Black History Month, National Cherry Month, National Condom Month, National Mend A Broken Heart Month, National Parent Leadership Month, National Pet Dental Health Month, National Teen Dating Violence Awareness and Prevention Month, National Time Management Month, Plant the Seeds of Greatness Month, Return Shopping Carts to the Supermarket Month, Spay/Neuter Awareness Month, Spunky Old Broads Month, Wise Health Care Consumer Month, Worldwide Renaissance of the Heart Month, Youth Leadership Month

WEEK-LONG HOLIDAYS

Feb 1 – 7 African Heritage and Health Week

Feb 1 – 12 Japan: Sapporo Snow Festival

Feb 2 – 19 Canada: Winterlude

Feb 4 – 10 Children's Authors and Illustrators Week,

Feb 5 – 9 International Networking Week

Feb 8 – 14 Love Makes the World Go Round; but, Laughter Keeps Us from Getting Dizzy Week

Feb 9 – 11 Gold Rush Days

Feb 11 – 13 Shrovetide

Feb 11 – 17 International Flirting Week, Random Acts of Kindness Week

Feb 12 – 13 Carnival, Fasching

Feb 12 – 17 Freelance Writers Appreciation Week

Feb 12 – 18 Love a Mensch Week

Feb 13 – 15 World AG Expo

Feb 16 – 19 Great Backyard Bird Count

Feb 18 – 24 Build a Better Trade Show Image Week

Feb 25 – Mar 3 National Eating Disorders Awareness Week, Telecommuter Appreciation Week

DAILY HOLIDAYS

1. Car Insurance Day, Freedom Day, G. I. Joe Day, National Candy-Making Day, *Robinson Crusoe Day

2. American Dental Association Give Kids a Smiley Day, *Bonza Bottler Day™, Bubble Gum Day, *Candelmas, *Groundhog Day, *Hedgehog Day, *Imbolic Sled Dog Day, Mexico: Dia de la Candelaria, National Wear Red Day, The Record of a Sneeze Day (125th Anniversary)

3. *Four Chaplains Memorial Day, *The Day, The Music Died Day (1959), *Income Tax Birthday, Japan: Bean Throwing Festival Day (Setsubun), Take Your Child to the Library Day, Vietnam: National Holiday

4. *Facebook Launch Day (2004), Lindbergh Day, Medjool Date Day, *Rosa Parks Birthday (1913), Sri Lanka: Independence Day, Switzerland: Homstom, *USO Day, World Cancer Day

5. *Family Leave Bill (1993), Longest War in History Ends (1985), Mexico: Constitution Day, Move Hollywood and Broadway to Lebanon, Switzerland: Homstrom, *Weatherperson's Day

6. Accession of Queen Elizabeth II (1952), African–American Coaches Day, New Zealand: Waitangi Day, United Nations: International Day of Zero Tolerance for Female Genital Mutilation

7. *Ballet Day, *Chaplin's "Tramp" Day (1914), *Charles Dickens (1812), Granada: Independence Day, National Black HIV/AIDS Awareness Day, National Girls and Women in Sports Day, *Wave All Your Fingers at Your Neighbor's Day

8. *Boy Scouts of America Day (1910), Japan: Ha-Ri-Ku-Yo (Needle Mass), Opera Debut in the Colonies Day (1735), Slovenia: Culture Day

9. *Ernest Tubb (1914), *Gypsy Rose Lee (1914), Lebanon: St. Maron's Day, National Bagel Day, Read in a Bathtub Day, Union Officers Escape Libby Prison (1864)

10. *"All the News That's Fit to Print" Day, *Charles Lamb (1775), *First Computer Chess Victory over Human (1996), *First WWII Medal of Honor (1942), *Plimsoll Day, Treaty of Paris (1763)

11. Cameroon: Youth Day, Fasching Sunday, *First Woman Episcopal Bishop (1989), Get Out Your Guitar Day, *Japan: National Foundation Day, Man Day, Mandela Released Day (1990), *National Shut-in Visitation Day, *Pro Sports Wives Day, *Satisfied Staying Single Day, *Thomas Alva Edison Birthday (1847), United Nations: International Day of Women and Girls in Science, White Shirt Day

12. *Darwin Day, *Dracula Day, *Abraham Lincoln (1809) and Birthplace Cabin Wreath Laying Day, Iceland: Bun Day, Myanmar: Union Day, NAACP Day (1909), *Oglethorpe Day, *Safetypup's® Day, Shrove Monday

13. *Employee Legal Awareness Day, *First Magazine Published (1741), *Get a Different Name Day, International Pancake Day, *Madly In Love With Me Day, Mardi Gras, National Wingman's Day, Paczki Day, Shrove Tuesday, World Radio Day

14. Ash Wednesday, ENIAC Computer Day, *Ferris Wheel Day, *First Presidential Photograph Day (1849), *League of Women Voters Day, National Donor Day, *National Have-a-Heart Day, New Mexico: Extraterrestrial Culture Day, Race Relations Day, *Saint Valentine's Day

15. Afghanistan: Soviet Troop Withdrawal (1989), Asteroid Near Miss Day, Canada: Family Day and Maple Leaf Flag Day, *Chelyabinsk Meteor Explosion (5th Anniversary), *Galileo, Galilei (1564), *Lupercalia, *Remember the Maine Day, *Susan B. Anthony Day

16. 1Chinese New Year, Lithuania: Independence Day

17. *League of United Latin American Citizens (LULAC) Founded (1929), *My Way Day, *National PTA Founders Day, Random Acts of Kindness Day

18. Gambia: Independence Day, Helen Gurley Brown Day, Luxembourg: Bürgsonndeg, Nepal: National Democracy Day, Orthodox Forgiveness Sunday (Cheesefare Sunday), *Pluto (Planet) Day

19. Canada: Family Day (Selected Provinces), *Japanese Internment Day, Orthodox Green Monday, Presidents' Day, Washington's Birthday Observed

20. Ansel Adams Day (1925), Closest Approach of a Comet to Earth (1941), *Northern Hemisphere Hoodie Hoo Day (At high noon everyone yells "HoodiE-Hoo" to chase away winter and make way for spring.), *United Nations: World Day for Social Justice, World Pangolin Day

21. Bangladesh: Martyrs Day, Erma Bombeck Day (1927), CIA Agent Arrested as Spy Day (1994), *United Nations: International Mother Language Day, *Washington Monument Dedicated (1885)

22. Digital Learning Day, Discovere Girl Day, *George Washington's Birthday (1732), Montgomery Boycott Arrests Day (1956), National Chili Day, Saint Lucia: Independence Day, Woolworth's Day (1879)

23. Brunei Darussalam: National Day, *Curling is Cool Day, Diesel Engine Day, First Cloning of an Adult Animal (1997), Guyana: Anniversary of Republic, *Iwo Jima Day (flag raised), Russia: Defender of the Fatherland Day, Single Tasking Day

24. Estonia: Independence Day, Gregorian Calendar Day (1582), Mexico: Flag Day, National Dance Day, Open That Bottle Night, Steve Jobs Birthday (1955), *Wilhelm Carl Grimm (1786), World Sword Swallower's Day

25. *Jim Backus Birthday (1913), Kuwait: National Day

26. Buffalo Bill Cody Day (1846), *Federal Communications Commission Created (FCC), (1934), *For Pete's Sake Day, Kuwait: Liberation Day, *Levi Strauss Day

27. Dominican Republic: Independence Day, *Henry Wadsworth Longfellow Birthday (1807), International Polar Bear Day, Travel Africa Day, Twenty-Second Amendment to US Constitution Ratification (1951), World Spay Day

28. Floral Design Day, Inconvenience Yourself™ Day, *National Tooth Fairy Day, Taiwan: Peace Memorial Day

HOLIDAY MARKETING IDEAS FOR FEBRUARY

National Time Management Month —This is one thing we all struggle with. Time managed properly allows you to complete your projects on time and still have time and energy to spend doing the other things you so much enjoy. So, as you look to how to celebrate National Time Management Month consider events, cards, or daily words of advice posted on your social media channels. How about a YouTube video where you give helpful time management times? Remember, you have a whole month, so there's no excuse not to manage your time wisely and promote your business in the process.

Feb 6 African–American Coaches Day —Imagine crossing the cultural divide and helping each other. Why not host an online event and invite your friends to join you as celebrate our African-American brothers and sisters who have struggled to break their own proverbial 'glass ceiling'? While your speakers don't all have to be ethnic, perhaps the topics could cover issues pertinent to the struggles they face. If you take the time to survey the audience, you may even be able to get to the root of their issues during your online event.

Feb 11 Get Out Your Guitar Day — It's time to make your world ROCK! Whether you are musically inclined or not, today you can promote your business with a song. Don't 'fret' you're sure to enjoy this weird & wacky holiday. One easy idea is to send out cards. Another would be to post videos or snaps of your favorite guitar player. If you do the videos or snaps, you might generate some interest by adding a puzzle or quiz about the artist. Another option is to host a live Facebook if you are up to the challenge and happen to be able to strum the wires yourself. Be sure to look in the Samples Appendix for a flyer you can freely use.

Feb 13 Get a Different Name Day — Have you always wanted to have a different nom de plume? Today is your day to make your wish come true. I can easily think of two good choices to celebrate this weird & wacky holiday. The first is to grab a nametag and put your favorite moniker on it and display it proudly. When asked, be sure to let others know that you are celebrating today. The second would be to gather a group and swap name tags and see who comes up with the most correctly swapped. Put a time limit on it and let the fun begin. This is most amusing with a group where not everyone knows each other.

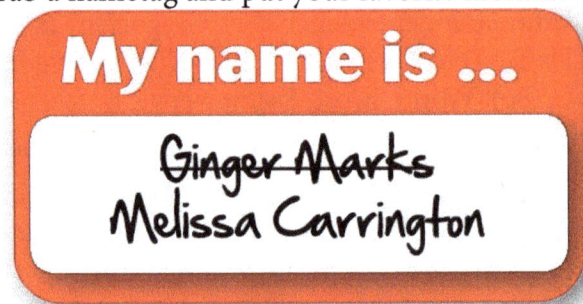

My name is ...

~~Ginger Marks~~
Melissa Carrington

Feb 20 World Pangolin Day — Put on your conservation gloves and roll up your sleeves today as we look to the most illegally traded species on the planet, the pangolin. Also known as the scaly anteater it resides in Africa and Asia. There are eight species, two of which may go extinct within only 10 years! Born Free USA has a free downloadable poster you can share on your social media. You'll find the link in the appendix. Share the awareness by getting involved with social media posts or create simple pangolin day stickers to hand out to those you meet along your way. You'll find a design to get you on the right track in the appendix.

Feb 26 For Pete's Sake Day— We've all at least thought this saying at least once in our lives. Well, today you can actually verbalize it. Who the heck is Pete anyway? Why not for Patricia's sake? Create a countdown clock and put it on your website just for the fun of it (you'll find a link to a creation tool in the appendix). If you want to send out cards, there is a cute one available at Greeting Card Universe. You'll find their link in the appendix as well as a link that explains the origin of this weird & wacky holiday. Oh, and be sure to wish everyone a happy For Pete's Sake Day!

MARCH

MONTH-LONG HOLIDAYS

Mar 3 – 20 Iditarod Trail Sled Dog Race
Mar 13 – Apr 15 Deaf History Month
Mar 18 – 31 Passiontide

Alport Syndrome Awareness Month, American Red Cross Month, Colorectal Cancer Awareness Month, Credit Education Month, Employee Spirit Month, Humorists Are Artists Month, International Black Women in Jazz Month, International Ideas Month, International Mirth Month, Irish-American Heritage Month, Music in our Schools Month, National Clean Up Your IRS Act Month, National Colorectal Cancer Awareness Month (Different sponsor from Colorectal Cancer Awareness Month), National Craft Month, National Eye Donor Month, National Kidney Month, National Multiple Sclerosis Education and Awareness Month, National Nutrition Month®, National Peanut Month, National Umbrella Month, National Women's History Month, Optimism Month, Paws to Read Month, Play the Recorder Month, Poison Prevention Awareness Month, Red Cross Month, Save the Vaquita Month, Save Your Vision Month, Sing with Your Child Month, Social Work Month, Women's History Month, Workplace Eye Wellness Month, Youth Art Month

WEEK-LONG HOLIDAYS

Mar 1 – 7 Will Eisner Week

Mar 1 – 4 Emerald City Comicon

Mar 1 – 11 Florida Strawberry Festival

Mar 1 – 14 Japan: Omizutori (Water-Drawing Festival)

Mar 2 – 3 Texas Cowboy Poetry Gathering

Mar 2 – 4 Aldo Leopold Weekend, International Festival of Owls

Mar 2 – 6 CAMEX

Mar 4 – 10 Celebrate Your Name Week, National Consumer Protection Week, Professional Pet Sitters Week, Return the Borrowed Books Week, Teen Tech Week

Mar 5 – 9 National School Breakfast Week

Mar 7 – 10 Association of Writers and Writing Programs Conference and Bookfair (Tampa, FL)

Mar 8 – 15 HeForShe Arts Week

Mar 9 – 10 National Day of Unplugging

Mar 9 – 18 England: Words by the Water: A Festival of Words and Ideas

Mar 11 – 17 Termite Awareness Week

Mar 12 – 18 Brain Awareness Week, United Kingdom: Shakespeare Week

Mar 16 – 18 Sherlock Holmes Weekend

Mar 17 – 18 Military Through the Ages

Mar 18 – 24 Consider Christianity Week, National Poison Prevention Week, Passion Week, World Folk Tales and Fables Week

Mar 19 – 25 Act Happy Week, National Animal Poison Prevention Week, Wellderly Week

Mar 21 – 27 United Nations: Week of Solidarity with the Peoples Struggling Against Racism and Racial Discrimination

Mar 23 – 25 American Crossword Puzzle Tournament

Mar 25 – 31 Greece: Dumb Week, Holy Week, National Protocol Officers' Week,

Mar 26 – 29 Italy: Bologna Children's Book Fair

Mar 31 – Apr 7 Pesach or Passover

DAILY HOLIDAYS

1. Baby Sleep Day, Bosnia and Herzegovina: Independence Day, *Iceland: Beer Day, Korea: Samiljol or Independence Movement Day, Korea: Samiljol or Independence Movement Day, Landmine Ban Day, *National Pig Day, Paraguay: National Heroes' Day, *Peace Corps Founded (1961), Plan a Solo Vacation Day, Purim, *Refired, Not Retired Day, Switzerland: Chalandrea Maraz, United Kingdom and Ireland: World Book Day, Wales: Saint David's Day, World Compliment Day, Zero Discrimination Day

2. China, Taiwan, Korea: Lantern Festival, Dress in Blue Day, Ethiopia: Adwa Day, *Highway Numbers Day, *King Kong Premier (1933), NEA's Read Across America Day, World Day of Prayer

3. Alexander Graham Bell (1847), *Bonza Bottler Day™, Bulgaria: Liberation Day, International Ear Care Day, Japan: Hina Matsuri (Doll Festival), Malawi: Martyr's Day, *National Anthem Day (1931), Simplify-Your-Life Day, United Nations: World Wildlife Day, *What If Cats and Dogs Had Opposable Thumbs Day, World Birth Defects Day

4. Courageous Follower Day, Namesake Day, *National Grammar Day, Old Inauguration Day

5. Australia: Eight Hour Day or Labor Day, Fun Facts About Names Day, Guam: Discovery Day or Magellan Day, National Poutine Day, Saint Piran's Day, Unites States Bank Holiday, World Tennis Day

6. *Dred Scott Day, Ghana: Independence Day, *Michelangelo (1475), Peace Corp Day, Town Meeting Day, Unique Names Day

7. Discover What Your Name Means Day, Suez Canal Day

8. International Working Women's Day, Nametag Day, National Proofreading Day, Registered Dietitian Nutritionists Day, Russia: International Women's Day, Syrian Arab Republic: Revolution Day, United Nations: International Women's Day, United States Income Tax (1913), World Kidney Day

9. *Barbie Day, Belize: Baron Bliss Day, Middle Name Pride Day, Panic Day, Shabbat Across America and Canada, Saint Frances of Rome: Feast Day, Vespucci Day

10. Genealogy Day, International Bagpipe Day, International Fanny Pack Day, *Mario Day, National Women and Girls HIV/AIDS Awareness Day, *Salvation Army Day, *Telephone Invention Day, *US Paper Money Day

11. Check Your Batteries Day, Daylight Savings Time Begins, Dream Day 2018, England: Mothering Sunday, *Johnny Appleseed Day, Lithuania: Restitution of Independence Day

12. *FDR's First Fireside Chat (1933), Fill Our Staplers Day (also Nov 5), Gabon: National Day, *Girl Scout Day, Great Blizzard Day, Moshoeshoe's Day, Mauritius: Independence Day, National Napping Day, United Kingdom: Commonwealth Day

13. *Earmuffs Day, Good Samaritan Involvement Day, National Open an Umbrella Indoors Day, Smart and Sexy Day

14. *Albert Einstein Birthday (1879), Moth-er Day, Pi Day (as in the math pie = 3.14159265 etc.), Registered Dietitian Nutritionist Day, "10 Most Wanted List" Day

15. Absolutely Incredible Kid Day, Brutus Day, Ides of March, True Confessions Day

16. *Black Press Day (1827), Curlew Day, Freedom of Information Day, Goddard Day, *Lips Appreciation Day, National Panda Day, No Selfies Day

17. *Campfire USA Day, Ireland: National Day, National Quilting Day, Play the Recorder Day, Saint Patrick's Day, Save the Florida Panther Day

18. Aruba: Flag Day, Forgive Mom and Dad Day, *National Biodiesel Day

19. Australia: Canberra Day, Iran: National Day of Oil, Saint Joseph's Day, Swallows Return to San Juan Capistrano Day, US Standard Time Act (100th Anniversary), *Wyatt Earp (1848)

20. *Great American Meat Out Day, Iranian New Year (Noruz), National Agriculture Day, Ostara, *Proposal Day®, Snowman Burning, Tunisia: Independence Day, *United Nations: International Day of Happiness, *Won't You Be My Neighbor Day

21. *Bach Day, *First Round-the-World Balloon Flight (1999), Lesotho: National Tree Planting Day, Memory Day, Namibia: Independence Day, National Healthy Fats Day, Naw-Ruz, South Africa: Human Rights Day, *Twitter Day, *United Nations: International Day for the Elimination of Racial Discrimination, United Nations: International Day of Forests, United Nations: World Poetry Day, World Down Syndrome Day

22. As Young As You Feel Day, India: New Year's Day, *International Day of The Seal, *Louis L'Amour Day (1908), Laser Patented Day (1960), *National Goof-off Day, United Nations: World Day for Water (aka World Water Day)

23. Beat the Clock Day, "Big Bertha Paris Gun Day, *Liberty Day, National Puppy Day, National Tamale Day, *Near Miss Day, "OK" Day, *United Nations: World Meteorological Day

24. Argentina: National Day of Memory for Truth and Justice, Be Mad Day, Earth Hour, Exxon Valdez Oil Spill (1989), *Houdini Day (1874), Philippine Independence, United Nations:

International Day for the Right to the Truth Concerning Gross Human Rights Violations and for the Dignity of Victims, *World Tuberculosis Day

25. *Bed In for Peace Day, European Union: Daylight Savings Time (Summertime begins), *Greece: Independence Day: National Day of Celebration of Greek and American Democracy, Maryland Day, National Medal of Honor Day, *Old New Year's Day, Palm Sunday, Pecan Day, Tolkien Reading Day, United Nations: International Day of Remembrance of The Victims of Slavery and The Transatlantic, United Nations: International Day of Solidarity with Detained and Missing Staff Members

26. Bangladesh: Independence Day, Camp David Accord Day, *Legal Assistants Day, Live Long and Prosper Day, *Make Up Your Own Holiday Day, Seward's Day

27. American Diabetes Association Alert Day, Education and Sharing Day (tentative), *FDA Approves Viagra Day, *Quirky Country Music Song Titles Day

28. Czech Republic: Teachers' Day, Whole Grain Sampling Day

29. *Canada: British North America Act (1867), Central African Republic: Boganda Day, Dow Jones Day, *Knights of Columbus Founders Day, *National Mom and Pop Business Owner's Day, *Niagara Falls Runs Dry (1848), Pearl Bailey Day (100th Anniversary), Taiwan: Youth Day, *Texas Loves the Children Day

30. Anesthetic Day, *Doctors Day, Good Friday, Grass is Always Browner on the Other Side of the Fence Day, Passover (begins at sundown), *Pencil Day, Vincent Van Gogh Day (1853), World Bipolar Day

31. *Bunsen Burner Day, Cesar Chavez Day, Easter Even, *Eiffel Tower Day (1998), International Hug a Medievalist Day, Lazarus Saturday, *National "She's Funny That Way" Day, World Backup Day

HOLIDAY MARKETING IDEAS FOR MARCH

National Umbrella Month — April showers are coming next month. So, it's time to celebrate the handy device that has saved countless hairdos. While thinking of ways to celebrate the first thing that comes to mind is a coloring or cute photo contest. Your umbrella art can be as colorful and ornate or as stoic as the trusty solid black. Add fringe or not, the only rule is to have fun creating your own National Umbrella Month contest and when April showers roll around you can announce the winner. You'll find a coloring page in the appendix.

For the faint at heart you could always just send out rain day cards. Remember, a real card is better than an e-card, but an e-card is better than nothing.

Another idea is to organize a National Umbrella Month charity event. First, you'll probably want to get sponsors. Then, purchase only one color of umbrellas, for example red, orange, or yellow. During the month make them available at different businesses, retail stores, or online. The money from the sales could go to children at risk to help

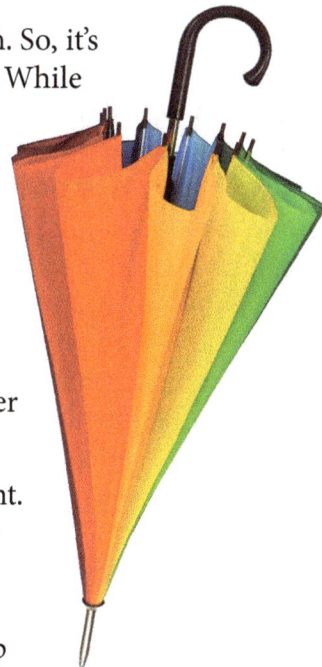

with after school programs or food and clothing. If you decide to tackle this project, be sure to get your city involved and let the media know your plans. You can be sure they'll help spread the word!

May 3 International Ear Care Day — What do Q-tips® and ears have in common? Nothing! Ask your ear doctor and they'll tell you there are some things you should never put in your ears and Q-tips are one of them. On this weird & wacky holiday one of the best ways to celebrate is to give out Ear Care Day fact sheets. You can also post tips on social media or even create a Facebook Live video. There are numerous ways to honor our ears today including listening, at a reasonable decibel. Gather a group and share advice on subjects of interest to your customers and contacts. If you want a quick fact sheet, look in the appendix. You'll find one there that I have designed for you.

May 10 Telephone Invention Day — Where would we be without this device? We use it every day. It's not just for making phone calls anymore. Now we text, surf the internet, and even do our banking on these handy devices. So much a part of our daily lives is consumed with the use of them that we must not miss the opportunity to call this weird & wacky holiday to the forefront of your attention. To celebrate this holiday, grab a couple of cans and some string and make your very own 'telephone'. You'll find the instructions in the appendix, if you have forgotten how.

If you really want to put this holiday to the best use, try picking up your favorite phone device and calling your customers and clients to let them know how important they are to you. Thank them for their loyalty and perhaps they will think of something they need you to assist them with.

Mar 21 Memory Day — Before you know it this day will be just a memory. So, fire up those synapses and put your memory to good use. Brain games that test your memory are a good place to start. If you have the time and inclination, you might even host an event with a theme of memory loss prevention. As we are fast becoming an elderly generation, Alzheimer's and dementia are growing problems. Why not spend the day educating folks or visiting your local nursing home? They may not remember your visit, but you will. And, since poetry has a profound impact on people with these ailments you might even consider memory day poetry contest. Be sure to visit The Poetry Archive to listen to some poems for inspiration. You'll find the link in the appendix.

NATIONAL MEMORY DAY
Poetry Collection

APRIL

MONTH-LONG HOLIDAYS

Adopt a Ferret Month, Alcohol Awareness Month, Black Women's History Month, Community Spirit Days, Couple Appreciation Month, Defeat Diabetes Month, Distracted Driving Awareness Month, Grange Month, Holy Humor Month, Informed Women Month, International Customer Loyalty Month, International Twit Award Month, Jazz Appreciation Month, Library Snapshot Days, Mathematics Awareness Month, Month of the Young Child®, National African-American Women's Fitness Month, National Autism Awareness Month, National Cancer Control Month, National Card and Letter Writing Month, National Child Abuse Prevention Month, National Decorating Month, National Donate Life Month, National Exchange Club Child Abuse Prevention Month, National Humor Month, National Knuckles Down Month, National Lawn Care Month, National Occupational Therapy Month, National Pecan Month, National Pest Management Month, National Poetry Month, National Rebuilding Month, National Sexual Assault Awareness Month, Nationally Sexually Transmitted Diseases (STDs) Month, National Soy Foods Month, National Youth Sports Safety Month, Pet First Aid Awareness Month, Pharmacists War on Diabetes Month, Prevention of Animal Cruelty Month, Rosacea Awareness Month, School Library Month, Straw Hat Month, Stress Awareness Month, Women's Eye Health and Safety Month, Workplace Conflict Awareness Month, World Landscape Architecture Month, Worldwide Bereaved Spouses Awareness Month

WEEK-LONG HOLIDAYS

Apr 1–7 Laugh at Work Week, Orthodox Holy Week, Testicular Cancer Awareness Week (aka Get a Grip Day)

Apr 2–7 Explore Your Career Options Week

Apr 4–10 Hate Week —"Down with Big Brother"

Apr 6–8 Chicago Comic and Entertainment Expo (C2E2)

Apr 7–8 Just Pray No! Worldwide Weekend of Prayer and Fasting

Apr 8–14 National Crime Victims' Rights Week, National Library Week, Pan–American Week

Apr 10–12 London Book Fair

Apr 14–22 National Park Week

Apr 15–21 National Coin Week

Apr 15–22 National Volunteer Week

Apr 21 – 28 Money Smart Week®, Administrative Professionals Week

Apr 22 – 28 Chemists Celebrate Earth Week, International Dark Sky Week, Preservation Week, Sky Awareness Week

Apr 23 – 27 National Playground Safety Week

Apr 26 – 29 Fiddler's Frolics

Apr 29 – May 5 Japan: Golden Week Days

DAILY HOLIDAYS

1. *April Fool's or All Fool's Day, Bulgaria: St Lasarus' Day, Mylesday, Palm Sunday, Reading is Funny Day, *Sorry Charlie Day, US Air Force Academy Day

2. Casanova Day, Dyngus Day USA, Easter Monday, Hans Christian Anderson Day (1805), *International Children's Book Day, *Sir Alec Guinness (1914), Love Your Produce Manager Day, National Ferret Day, Ponce de Leon Discovers Florida (1513), *Reconciliation Day, *United Nations: World Autism Awareness Day, US Mint Day

3. Blacks Ruled Eligible to Vote Day (1944), *Pony Express Day, National Weed Out Hate: Sow the Seeds of Peace Day, *Tweed Day

4. *Beatles Take Over Music Charts (1964), *Bonza Bottler Day™, Flag Act of 1818 Day, Senegal: Independence Day, Taiwan: Children's Day, *United Nations: International Day for Mine Awareness and Assistance in Mine Action, *Vitamin C Day

5. Gold Star Spouses Day, *Helen Keller's Miracle Day, National Alcohol Screening Day, National Deep Dish Pizza Day

6. International Kids Yoga Day, North Pole Discovery Day, *Tartan Day, *Teflon Day (1938), Thailand: Chakri Day, United Nations: International Day of Sport for Development and Peace

7. *International Beaver Day, International Pillow Fight Day, International Snailpapers Day, *Metric System Day, National Beer Day (1933), National Love Your Children Day, *No Housework Day, United Nations: International Day of the Reflection on the Genocide in Rwanda, *United Nations: World Health Day

8. Home Run Record Set by Hank Aaron (1974), International Roma Day, Japan: Flower Festival (Hana Matsuri), National Dog Fighting Awareness Day

9. *Civil Rights Bill of 1866 Day, Civil War Ends (1865), *Jenkins Ear Day, Jumbo the Elephant Day, National Former Prisoner of War Recognition Day, *Winston Churchill Day

10. ASPCA Incorporation Day (1866), Children's Day in Florida (always the second Tuesday), *Commodore Perry Day, International Be Kind to Lawyers Day, National Library Workers Day, *National Siblings Day, *Safety Pin Day, *Salvation Army Founder's Day

11. *Barbershop Quartet Day, Civil Rights Act Day (1968), *International "Louie Louie" Day, National Bookmobile Day

12. Halifax: Independence Day, *National D.E.A.R. Day (aka Drop Everything and Read), *National Licorice Day, Polio Vaccine Day, Truancy Day, United Nations: International Day of Human Space Flight, *Walk on Your Wild Side Day, Yuri's Night

13. Blame Someone Else Day, Friday the Thirteenth, *Guy Fawkes Day, *Thomas Jefferson Day

14. *Children with Alopecia Day, India: Vaisakhi, *International Moment of Laughter Day, Pan American Day, Pan–American Day, Pathologists' Assistant Day

15. Boston Marathon Bombing (2013), Botox Day, *Deaf School Day, *McDonald's Day, *Income Tax Pay Day — But Not this Year, National Auctioneers Day, *National Take a Wild Guess Day, *National That Sucks Day, Record Store Day, *Titanic Sinking (1912)

16. Boston Marathon, *Charlie Chaplin Day (1889), Emancipation Day, Income Tax Pay Day — This is Really It, Quarterly Estimated Federal Income Tax Payers' Due Date (also Jan 15, Jun 15, and Sep 17, 2018)

17. American Samoa: Flag Day, *Blah! Blah! Blah! Day, *Ellis Island Family History Day, Herbalist Day, International Haiku Poetry Day, National Stress Awareness Day, Syrian Arab Republic: Independence Day

18. Canada: Constitution Act of 1982, The House that Ruth Built Day, *International Amateur Radio Day, Paul Revere's Ride Day (1775), *Pet Owners Independence Day, "Third World" Day, Zimbabwe: Independence Day

19. Branch Davidian Fire at Waco (1993), John Parker Day, National Hanging Out Day, National High Five Day, Oklahoma City Bombing (1995), Patriots Day in Florida, Get to Know Your Customers Day (third Thursday of each quarter is set aside to get to know your customers even better)

20. National Teach Children to Save Day

21. Aggie Muster Day, Brazil: Tiradentes Day, *Kindergarten Day, National Bulldogs are Beautiful Day, Record Store Day, San Jacinto Day

22. Brazil Day, Coins Stamped "In God We Trust" Day, *Earth Day, *National Jelly Bean Day, Oklahoma Land Rush Day (1889), United Nations: International Mother Earth Day

23. Canada: Newfoundland: Saint George's Day, *Confederate Memorial Day, *Movie Theatre Day, *Public School Day, National English Muffin Day, Saint George Feast Day, Spain: Book Day and Lover's Day, Turkey: National Sovereignty and Children's Day, William Shakespeare Day (1564), United Nations: English Language Day, *United Nations: World Book and Copyright Day, World Book Night

24. Ireland: Easter Rising (1916), Library of Congress Day

25. Abortion Legalized (1967), Administrative Professionals Day or Secretary's Day, Anzac Day, Egypt: Sinai Day, *License Plates Day, Swaziland: National Flag Day, World Malaria Day, World Penguin Day, East Meets West Day

26. Audubon Day, Florida and Georgia: Confederate Memorial Day, *Hug an Australian Day, National Help a Horse Day, National Pretzel Day, *Richter Scale Day, Take Our Daughters and Sons to Work® Day (fourth Thursday in April), United Nations: International Chernobyl Disaster Remembrance Day, United Nations: World Intellectual Property Day

27. Arizona: Arbor Day, *Babe Ruth Day (1947), Mantanzas Mule Day, *Morse Code Day, Most Tornadoes in a Day (US), National Arbor Day, National Hairball Awareness Day, National Little Pampered Dog Day, Sierra Leon: Independence Day, Togo: Independence Day

28. Biological Clock Gene Discovered (1994), Canada: National Day of Mourning, National Rebuilding Day, United Nations: World Day for Safety and Health at Work, Workers Memorial Day, World Healing Day, World Tai Chi and Qigong Day, World Veterinary Day

29. Japan: Showa Day, Mother, Father Deaf Day, *"Peace" Rose Day, Switzerland: Landsgemeinde, United Nations: Day of Remembrance for all Victims of Chemical Warfare, Zipper Day (1913), Zipper Day

30. Beltane, Birthday of Buddha, *Bugs Bunny Day (1938), Día de los Niños/Día de los Libros, International Jazz Day, National Animal Advocacy Day, National Honesty Day (Honest Abe Awards), *Spank Out Day USA, Vietnam: Liberation Day, *Walpurgis Night

HOLIDAY MARKETING IDEAS FOR APRIL

National Knuckles Down Month — Whilst knuckles down is a saying we have heard at one time or another, this holiday is all about marbles. It is a position that you place your knuckle when shooting. That being said, the phrase is the way to play this holiday month out. Events are the way to go. Anything having to do with improving your business is fair game. So, gather a group of speakers on subjects such as time management, social media, and marketing. When all the speakers help you promote your event you are sure to reach a circle of influence.

Apr 5 Gold Star Spouses Day — Today is a day dedicated to those widows/widowers whose spouses died while serving in the Armed Forces of the United States, or as result of service-connected disabilities. What better way to spend the day than to recognize these special men and women who have given their most beloved one in service to our country? To bring awareness in your community wear a badge of honor showing your support of the spouses of our fallen veterans. Be sure to post on social media and thank them for their sacrifice. I've designed a pin you can print and wear and a graphic you can use on your social media channels. You will find them in the appendix.

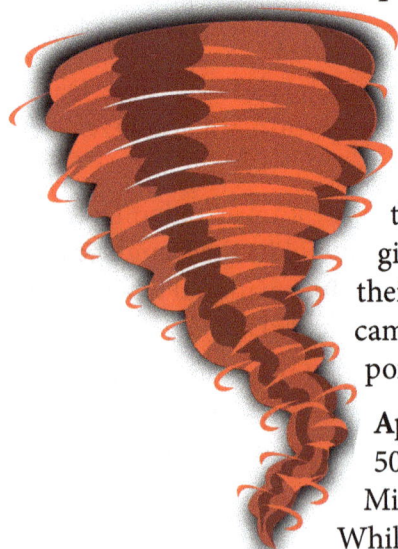

Apr 11 Barbershop Quartet Day — Barbershop quartets are no longer reserved for men. Women quartets have sung their way into our hearts as well. In honor of this weird & wacky holiday listen to some good old-fashioned barbershop or get some friends together and sing a few bars. This could also be a great time to plan an event with your local choruses and quartets — plan a joint rehearsal, throw a tag party, or just get together to celebrate Barbershop. If you give the singers the spotlight, be sure to have them tell you some of their stories. You'll be surprised at the diversity of ways these groups came to be. Consider making this a charity event and donating a portion of the ticket sales to a favorite charity.

Apr 27 Most Tornadoes in a Day — There have been 13 days with 500 or more tornadoes since modern records began in 1950. The Mississippi Valley up to the Ohio Valley has had the most of them. While May 25 tops the list, the only day surpassing 600 total tornadoes, with 603 as of the 1950-2015 period, April is still the leader on any one single day (April 27, 2011) given its tendency for super outbreaks. I don't know about you, but I can't begin to wrap my brain around those numbers!

How to celebrate? Stir up a storm of information and whirl some new ideas around in your head. Gather up a group and brainstorm ideas on how to build your businesses. Sometimes, just getting someone else to share ideas with you will open your mind to new ideas you had never even considered before.

MAY

MONTH-LONG HOLIDAYS

May 9 – 20 Cannes Film Festival
May 16 – Jun 14 Ramadan: The Islamic Month of Fasting
May 28 – Jun 3 Black Single Parent's Week

Asian/Pacific American Heritage Month, Asthma Awareness Month, Better Hearing and Speech Month, Fibromyalgia Education and Awareness Month, Gardening for Wildlife Month, Get Caught Reading Month, Gifts from the Garden Month, Global Civility Awareness Month, Haitian Heritage Month, Heal the Children Month, Healthy Vision Month, Huntington's Disease Awareness Month, International Mediterranean Diet Month, International Victorious Woman Month, Jewish American Heritage Month, Law Enforcement Appreciation Month in Florida, Melanoma/Skin Cancer Detection and Prevention Month, Mental Health Month, Motorcycle Safety Month, Mystery Month, National Allergy/Asthma Awareness Month, National Arthritis Awareness Month, National Barbecue Month, National Bike Month, National Foster Care Month, National Good Car-Keeping Month, National Hamburger Month, National Hepatitis Awareness Month, National Meditation Month, National Military Appreciation Month, National Osteoporosis Awareness and Prevention Month, National Photo Month, National Physical Fitness and Sports Month, National Preservation Month, National Salad Month, National Stroke Awareness Month, National Sweet Vidalia® Onion Month, National Vinegar Month, Older American's Month, React Month, Spiritual Literacy Month, Strike Out Strokes Month, Ultraviolet Awareness Month, Women's Health Care Month, Young Achievers/Leaders of Tomorrow Month

WEEK-LONG HOLIDAYS

May 1 – 7 Choose Privacy Week

May 6 – 12 Be Kind to Animals Week®, Goodwill Industries Week, National Family Week, National Hug Holiday Week, National Hurricane Preparedness Week, National Nurses Week, National Pet Week, Root Canal Awareness Week, Update Your References Week

May 7 – 11 PTA Teacher Appreciation Week

May 7 – 13 National Stuttering Awareness Week, National Wildflower Week

May 13 – 19 National Police Week, National Transportation Week

May 14 – 18 National Etiquette Week

May 14 – 20 Salute to 35+ Moms Week, Work at Home Moms Week

May 16–21 National Foul Ball Week

May 19–20 Fishing Has No Boundaries Days

May 19–25 National Safe Boating Week

May 20–26 International New Friends Old Friends Week, World Trade Week, National Unicycle Week

May 20–27 National African Violet Week

May 24–27 Memory Days,

May 21–28 National Backyard Games Week

May 30–Jun 1 BookExpo America

DAILY HOLIDAYS

1. *Amtrak, Executive Coaching Day, Great Britain Formed Day (1707), Hug Your Cat Day, Skyscraper Day, *Keep Kids Alive — Drive 25® Day, Labor Day, *Law Day, *Lei Day, *Loyalty Day, *May Day, May One Day, Mother Goose Day, National Bubba Day, *New Home Owners Day, *School Principals' Day, World Asthma Day

2. King James Bible Published Day, United Nations: World Tuna Day

3. Dow Jones Tops 11,000 Day (1999), *Garden Meditation Day, Japan: Constitution Memorial Day, Lag B'Omer, *Lumpy Rug Day, Mexico: Day of the Holy Cross, National Day of Prayer, National Day of Reason, National Public Radio Day, National Specially-Abled Pets Day, *National Two Different Colored Shoes Day, *United Nations: World Press Freedom Day

4. China: Youth Day, Curaçao: Memorial Day, Jamaica Discover Day (1494), *International Respect for Chickens Day, Italy: Giro D'Italia, Japan: Greenery Day, *Star Wars Day

5. AMA Founded Day (1847), *Bonza Bottler Day™, *Cartoonists Day, *Cinco de Mayo, Free Comic Book Day, International Day of the Midwife, Japan and South Korea: Children's Day, Kentucky Derby, National Auctioneers Day

6. *Joseph Brackett Day, Motorcycle Mass and Blessing of the Bikes, National Infertility Survival® Day, *No Diet Day, *No Homework Day, Rogation Sunday, Rural Life or Soil Stewardship Sunday, Orson Wells Day (1915)

7. Beaufort Scale Day, Dow Jones Tops 15000 (2013), Melanoma Monday

8. National Teacher Day, *No Socks Day, *United Nations: Time of Remembrance and Reconciliation WWII (8–9), *V E Day, *World Red Cross Red Crescent Day

9. Donate A Day's Wages to Charity Day, European Union Founded (1950), National Bike to School Day, National Nightshift/Thirdshift Workers Day, National Receptionists Day, National School Nurse Day

10. Ascension Day, Golden Spike Driving Day, Singapore: Day of Vesak, United Nations: World Migratory Bird Day, World Lupus Day

11. *Eat What You Want Day, Military Spouse Appreciation Day

12. International Migratory Bird Day, Jamestown Day, Letter Carriers' "Stamp Out Hunger" Food Drive, *Limerick Day, National Babysitters Day, Native American Rights Day (1879), *Odometer Day, Stay Up All Night Night, World Fair Trade Day

13. Children of Fallen Patriots Day, Mother's Day, Mother's Day at the Wall, National Hummus Day

14. Fahrenheit Day, *Lewis and Clark Expedition Sets Out Day (1804), Smallpox Vaccine Discovery (1796), *The Stars and Stripes Forever Day, *Underground America Day, WAAC Day (1942)

15. Flight Attendant Day, Hyperemesis Gravidarum Awareness Day, Japan: Aoi Matsuri (Hollyhock Festival), Mexico: San Isidro Day, Nakba Day, National Sliders Day, *Nylon Stockings Day, *Peace Officer Memorial Day, *United Nations: International Day of Families

16. *Academy Awards Day (1929), *Biographer's Day, *First Woman to Climb Mt Everest Day (1975)

17. *First Kentucky Derby Day (1875), New York Stock Exchange Founded (1792), Orthodox Ascension Day, *Same-Sex Marriages Day (2004), *United Nations: World Telecommunications and Information Society Day

18. Endangered Species Day, Fishing Has No Boundaries Day, Haiti: Flag and University Day, *International Museum Day, International Virtual Assistants Day, National Bike to Work Day, National Defense Transportation Day, National Pizza Party Day, *Visit Your Relatives Day, Teacher's Day in Florida

19. Armed Forces Day, *Boys Club Day, Dark Day in New England, National Hepatitis Testing Day, Preakness Stakes, Shavuot (begins at sundown), Turkey: Youth and Sports Day

20. *Amelia Earhart Atlantic Crossing Day (1932), *Eliza Doolittle Day, Lindbergh Flight (1927), Mecklenburg Day, Neighbor Day, Pentecost, Ride a Unicycle Day, Shavuot, *Weights and Measures Day, Whitsunday

21. *American Red Cross Founder's Day, Canada: Victoria Day, England: Dicing for Bibles, *I Need a Patch for That Day, *National Wait Staff Day, *United Nations: World Day for Cultural Diversity for Dialogue and Development, Whitmonday

22. *Canadian Immigrants' Day, Germany: Waldchestag (Forest Day), Mr. Rogers Neighborhood Day, *National Maritime Day, Strongest Earthquake in the 20th Century (1960), *United Nations: International Day for Biological Diversity, World Goth Day

23. *Bonnie and Clyde Death (1934), *International World Turtle Day®, United Nations: International day to End Obstetric Fistula

24. Belize: Commonwealth Day, Brooklyn Bridge Open (1883), *Brother's Day, Declaration of the Bab, Eritrea: Independence Day, International Tiara Day, Monaco: Grand Prix de Monaco, *Morse Code Day, National Eat More Fruits and Vegetables Day

25. African Freedom Day, *Ralph Waldo Emerson (1803), *Jessie Owens' Day, Jordan: Independence Day, *National Missing Children's Day, *National Tap Dance Day, Poetry Day in Florida, *Towel Day, United Nations: Week of Solidarity with Peoples of Non-Self-Governing Territories

26. Australia: Sorry Day, Georgia: Independence Day, John Wayne (1907), World Lindy Hop Day

27. *Cellophane Tape Day, First Flight into the Stratosphere (1931), *Golden Gate Bridge Day, Haiti: Mother's Day, Indianapolis 500-Mile Race, Orthodox Pentecost, Trinity Sunday

28. *Amnesty International Founded (1961), Memorial Day, Prayer for Peace Memorial Day, *Sierra Club Day, *Slugs Return from Capistrano Day

29. *Amnesty for Southern Rebels Day, *Mount Everest Summit Reached (1953), *United Nations: International Day of United Nations Peacekeepers

30. *First American Daily Newspaper Published (1783), *Indianapolis 500 Anniversary (1911), *Loomis Day, Memorial Day (Traditional), National Senior Health and Fitness Day, Saint Joan of Arc Feast Day

31. *Copyright Law Passed (1970), Corpus Christi, *United Nations: World No–Tobacco Day, *Walt Whitman Day, *What You Think Upon Grows Day

HOLIDAY MARKETING IDEAS FOR MAY

Gifts from the Garden Month — It's time to celebrate Mother Earth and her bounty. Whether that means flowers or produce, trees or bees, our gardens offer up a bounty that is sure to please and appease. As we look to how we can best use this month to our advantage for our businesses healthy eating tops the list. Are you a health coach, cookbook author, or nutritionist? This month is your time to shine. You'll find some super cool gifts for your garden or for your garden lover at Uncommon Goods. The link is in the appendix if you dig garden gifts.

Possible ideas are sending cards, cooking classes, recipe swaps, or even a progressive dinner party also known as a Round Robbin. Don't know what those are? Each household feeds all the guests just one course. Keep that up from appetizer to dessert. How Stuff Works offers up a simple explanation on how to host your party. You'll find the link and the instructions in the appendix.

May 1 Loyalty Day — By presidential proclamation every year since 1955 Loyalty Day is a special day for the reaffirmation of loyalty to the United States and for the recognition of the heritage of American freedom. This year as we put aside our differences, let us celebrate this day and the freedom we share and the value we enjoy because of it. To mark this auspicious occasion and market your business at the same time consider participating in a parade. Contact your city government and suggest they get involved and celebrate this very special day. Cards, of course are the easier thing to do, but imagine the fun and notoriety you will garner in your local community when you help to plan and sponsor your local Loyalty Day parade.

LOYALTY DAY
"Keeping America Proud"

May 8 No Socks Day — No pantyhose or socks of any kind should be donned on this weird & wacky holiday. Wiggle those toes, dig them into the carpet or sand, whatever the case may be for you. If you are in an office kick off your shoes and socks and free your feet from their confines. If you get funny looks, smile kindly and wish them a Happy No Socks Day! If you are up to it and enjoy the out of doors you might also participate in a sockless sport such as swimming, beach volleyball, judo or karate, or water skiing. If not, perhaps you'll be just as happy sitting at your computer, sockless of course, tweeting #nosocksday and sharing your beautifully manicured digits on social media.

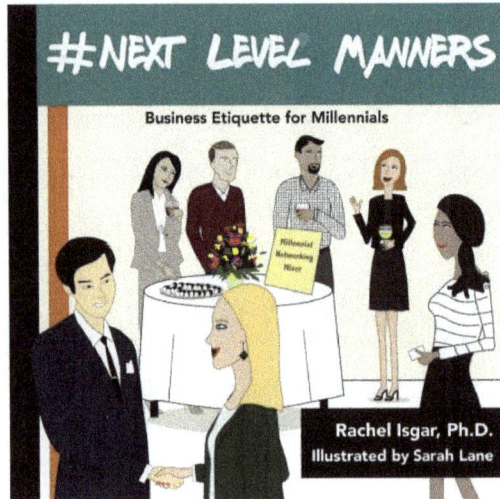

#NEXT LEVEL MANNERS

Business Etiquette for Millennials

Rachel Isgar, Ph.D.
Illustrated by Sarah Lane

May 14 – 18 National Etiquette Week—This is an area where many are lacking. Etiquette should not be a thing of the past! With the iPhone generation—and even some of us more mature business owners—while dining with others we find ourselves interrupted by our mobile phones. The easiest thing to do is to answer it, or at least look at it. Wouldn't it be better to turn it off and give your dinner partner your full attention (unless you are a doctor on call)? That's just an example of the poor etiquette of today's society at large. So, this week I suggest you start a pledge drive to practice better etiquette. You could put a pledge counter on your Facebook page or even your business website, especially if you have a career building or employment type of business.

Events are ideal as this is a week-long holiday. Why not host a Business Etiquette Dinner, speaker included? However, if you aren't up to that challenge, you could always send out a thank you card to your customers and clients. After all, that's proper etiquette too.

While researching this weird & wacky holiday I came across a book that you might want to give out copies as prizes or gifts at your event or keep on hand for your own enrichment. It is by Rachel Isgar, Ph.D. and is titled, #Next Level Manners: Business Etiquette for Millennials. You'll find the link in the appendix. She says, "…"

I have created a handout that you can brand with your business and hand out if you like. You'll find it in the samples section of the appendix.

May 21 I Need a Patch for That Day—We need patches every day. Every form and kind from patches in clothes to the nicotine and allergy patches, from software and tire patches to patchwork quilts. Patches hold us together and give useful items a longer more productive life. So, today we celebrate those patches that are so necessary to our very survival. In calling attention to this weird & wacky holiday consider patching together a clothing drive. Or, you could just pass out patches for all kinds of things like Willpower Patches and Eat Less Sugar Patches or even Procrastination Patches. You'll find some sample patches in the appendix that you can brand and create your own patches to hand out today.

JUNE

MONTH-LONG HOLIDAYS

Jun 1 – Nov 30 Atlantic, Caribbean and Gulf Hurricane Season
Jun 1 – Oct 31 Central Pacific Hurricane Season
Jun 30 – Jul 22 Tour de France

Adopt A Shelter Cat Month, African–American Music Appreciation Month, Audiobook Appreciation Month, Cancer From the Sun Month, Caribbean–American Heritage Month, Cataract Awareness Month, Child Vision Awareness Month, Dairy Alternative Month, Dementia Care Professionals Month, Effective Communications Month, Entrepreneurs and Do It Yourself Marketing Month, Fireworks Safety Month, Gay and Lesbian Pride Month, Great Outdoors Month, International Men's Month, International Surf Music Month, June Dairy Month, Perennial Gardening Month, GLBT (Gay, Lesbian, Bisexual and Transgender) Pride Month, Men's Health Education and Awareness Month, Migraine Awareness Month, National Aphasia Awareness Month, National Bathroom Reading Month, National Candy Month, National Caribbean–American Heritage Month, National GLBT Book Month, National Iced Tea Month, National Oceans Month, National Rivers Month, Nation Safety Month, National Soul Food Month, National Zoo and Aquarium Month, Pharmacists Declare War on Alcoholism Month, PTSD Awareness Month, Skyscraper Month, Sports America Kids Month, Student Safety Month

WEEK-LONG HOLIDAYS

Jun 2 – 3 Bookcon 2018 (Javits Center, NY, NY)

Jun 2 – 9 International Clothesline Week

Jun 3 – 9 Bed Bug Awareness Week, National Business Etiquette Week

Jun 10 – 16 National Flag Week

Jun 13 – 20 National Hermit Week

Jun 14 – 22 National Nursing Assistants Week

Jun 17 – 23 National Craft Spirits Week

Jun 18 – 24 Meet a Mate Week

Jun 20 – 23 International Listening Association Conference (Dublin, Ireland)

Jun 23 – 24 ARRL Field Day

Jun 24 – 30 Carpenter Ant Awareness Week,

Jun 29 – Jul 4 Freedom Days

Jun 30 – Jul 4 National Tom Sawyer Days

DAILY HOLIDAYS

1. Bahamas: Labor Day, China: International Children's Day, GM Bankruptcy (2009), *Heimlich Maneuver Day, National Donut Day, Say Something Nice Day, Superman Day, United Nations: Global Day of Parents

2. Italy: Republic Day, Marquis de Sade Birth (1740), National Gun Violence Awareness Day, National Trails Day, Saint Erasmus Day, United Kingdom: Coronation Day, *Yell Fudge at the Cobras in North America Day (Don't laugh, I haven't seen any lately!)

3. Children's Awareness Memorial Day, *Chimborazo Day, Confederate Memorial Day, Corpus Christi (US Observance), Japan: Day of the Rice God, *Mighty Casey Struck Out Day (1888), National Cancer Survivors Day, Spain: Baby Jumping Festival Day, Zoot Suit Riots Anniversary (75th Anniversary)

4. China: Tiananmen Square Massacre (1989), Finland: Flag Day, First Free Flight by a Woman (1784), Pulitzer Prize Day (1917), *United Nations: International Day of Innocent Children Victims of Aggression Day

5. *AIDS First Noted (1981), *Apple II (1977), Baby Boomers Recognition Day, *Hot Air Balloon Day (1783), *United Nations: World Environment Day

6. *Bonza Bottler Day™, *D–Day (1944), *Drive in Movie Day (1933), Global Running Day, Korea: Memorial Day, National Yo-yo Day, Prop 13 (40th Anniversary), *SEC Day (1934), Sweden: National Day

7. *(Daniel) Boone Day, Mackintosh Day, Malta: National Day, National Running Day, Supreme Court Strikes Down Connecticut Law Banning Contraception (1965)

8. First Heroine Woman Rewarded (1697), National Caribbean-American HIV/AIDS Awareness Day, *United Nations: World Ocean Day, *Upsy Daisy Day, World Oceans Day

9. Belmont Stakes Day, *Donald Duck Day, Family Health and Fitness Day (USA), International Archives Day

10. *AA Day (1935), American Mint Day (1652), *Ball Point Pen Day (1943), Children's Sunday, Multicultural American Child Awareness Day, Race Unity Day, Day of Portugal

11. Jacques Cousteau (1910), *Kamehameha Day (First Hawaiian King), National Cotton Candy Day, Queen's Official Birthday (Selected Nations)

12. *Baseball's First Perfect Game (1880), First Man-Powered Flight Across English Channel (1979), National Call Your Doctor Day, Loving v Virginia Day (1967), National Jerky Day, Orlando Nightclub Massacre (2016), Philippines: Independence Day, Russia: Russia Day, *"Tear Down This Wall" Day, United Nations: World Day Against Child Labor

13. Roller Coaster Day (1884), United Nations: International Albinism Awareness Day

14. Alzheimer Day, *Family History Day, First Nonstop Transatlantic Flight (1919), First US Breach of Promise Day, *Flag Day, Japan: Rice Planting Festival, UNIVAC Computer Day, US Army Day, World Blood Donor Day

15. *Magna Carta Day (1215), National Prune Day, Native American Citizenship Day, *Nature Photography Day, Quarterly Estimated Federal Income Tax Payers' Due Date (also Jan 15, Apr 16, and Sep 17, 2018), United Nations: World Elder Abuse Awareness Day, Work@Home Father's Day

16. *Bloomsday, House Divided Speech (1858), *Ladies' Day (Baseball), Longest Dam Race Day, South Africa: Youth Day, World Juggling Day

17. *Apartheid Day, Bunker Hill Day, Family Awareness Day, Father's Day, Husband Caregiver Day, Iceland: Independence Day, *United Nations: World Day to Combat Desertification and Drought

18. Battle of Waterloo Day, Korea: Swing Day, Egypt: Evacuation Day, Seychelles: Constitution Day, United Nations: Sustainable Gastronomy Day

19. Belmont Stakes Day, *Garfield the Cat Day (1978), *Juneteenth, Texas: Emancipation Day, United Nations: International Day for the Elimination of Sexual Violence in Conflict, "War is Hell" Day (1879), *World Sauntering Day

20. Argentina: Flag Day, *First Doctor of Science Earned by a Woman Day (1895), *United Nations: World Refugee Day

21. Anne and Samantha Day (also Dec 21), Go Skateboarding Day, Midsummer Day/Eve, Recess at Work Day, United Nations: International Day of Yoga, World Humanist Day, World Music Day/Fête de la Musique

22. Malta: Mnarja, National Eat at a Food Truck Day, Stupid Guy Thing Day, V-for Victory Day

23. Great American Backyard Campout Day, *Let It Go Day, Runner's Selfie Day, Typewriter Day, United Nations: International Widows Day, United Nations: Public Service Day

24. America's Kids Day, Canada: Saint John the Baptist Day, *Celebration of the Senses Day, China: Macau Day, "Flying Saucer" Day, Log Cabin Day, Saint John the Baptist Day, Singing on the Mountain Day,

25. Canada: Discover Day (Newfoundland and Labrador), Mozambique: Independence Day, Supreme Court Ruling Day (Bans School Prayer, Upholds Rights to Die), United Nations: Day of the Seafarer

26. *Barcode Day, CN Tower Day (1976), Federal Credit Union Act (1934), Human Genome Mapped (2000), National Columnists' Day, Saint Lawrence Seaway Dedication (1959), Supreme Court Strikes Down Defense of Marriage Act (2013), United Nations Charter Signing (1945), *United Nations: International Day Against Drug Abuse and Illicit Trafficking, *United Nations: International Day in Support of Victims of Torture

27. *Decide to be Married Day, *Happy Birthday to "Happy Birthday To You" Day, Industrial Workers of the World Day, *National HIV Testing Day, PTSD Awareness Day, United Nations: Micro-, Small-, and Medium-Sized Enterprises Day

28. Monday Holiday Law (1968), National Handshake Day, Treaty of Versailles (1919)

29. *Death Penalty Ban Day, Interstate Highway System Born (1956), Saint Peter and Paul Day, Saint Peter's Day, Seychelles: Independence Day

30. Asteroid Day, Britain Cedes Claim to Hong Kong (1997), Charles Blondin's Conquest of Niagara Falls (1859), Congo: Independence Day, Gone with the Wind Published (1936), *Leap Second Adjustment Time Day, *NOW (National Organization of Women) Founded (1966)

HOLIDAY MARKETING IDEAS FOR JUNE

Fireworks Safety Month —As we prepare for the big fireworks display on July 4th it seems appropriate to offer up this feature holiday for the month of June. If I may suggest a couple of marketing ideas; twitter and social media tips throughout the month, or a Fireworks Safety Month brochure, rack card, or flyer. Of course, you will want to brand it with your business information. You'll find a rack card you can use and make your own in the samples appendix.

Jun 2 – 9 International Clothesline Week — This week we are encouraged to bypass the electric or gas dryer in lieu of Mother Nature. However, clotheslines aren't just for hanging and adding the freshness that only Mother Nature can provide; you can hang anything from photos or artwork to mementos or plans or dreams. Spend this week helping others air out their visions. Why not find an accountability partner and brainstorm about your next goal and how you will reach it? Then follow-up to ensure you're keeping on track.

Another simple thing you can do is to snap a photo of your clothesline and share it on social media. If you are an author, you might have your readers take snaps of your book in different locations and place them on a virtual clothes line on Pinterest, Instagram, or Facebook. Coaches, retail or clothing stores, beauty products reps, candle makers, etc., you too can do the same.

Jun 18 United Nations: Sustainable Gastronomy Day — Today we seek to end poverty, protect the planet, and ensure prosperity for all. In doing so we all win. So, as you plan your business marketing around this weird & wacky holiday some things you could do are plan a cultural dinner or host a simple recipe swap. If you are up to the task, a food drive would be ideal! This is something the media would get behind and help you promote. Go for it! You'll be glad you did.

All the information on how to set-up and run your own food drive can be found on page 118 in the 2012 edition of this book followed by a food drive list that you may find helpful.

Jun 23 Let It Go Day — Okay, it's time. You've held onto that grudge or project quite long enough. It's time to let it go! If it ain't workin' try something else. One sure way to know if it isn't feasible is to step back and look at the obstacles that have gotten in the way. Are they challenges that made you stronger, or roadblocks to your success? Perhaps the best thing you can do today is to help others by hosting a Let It Go Day event. Invite speakers that specialize in career building, motivation, and procrastination. And, if all else fails, you have my permission to let it go and move on. You'll find a permission coin image that you can brand and hand out to all your attendees or clients in the samples appendix.

Jun 28 National Handshake Day — Your handshake speaks volumes. It can make or break a deal, or interview. So, if you are looking to market your business on this weird & wacky holiday I suggest you either have a live event or create videos to show the proper technique. Especially if you are a business or career coach or a recruiter, this is a superb day to showcase your professionalism and knowledge.

I have created a brochure that you can use to hand out to your attendees or clients. And, of course, you'll want to brand it to your business. If you need help doing so, send me a quick email to designer@documeantdesigns.com and I'll be happy to assist you.

JULY

MONTH-LONG HOLIDAYS

Jul 3 – Aug 11 Dog Days
Jul 3 – Aug 15 Air Conditioning Appreciation Days

Alopecia Month for Women, Bioterrorism/Disaster Education and Awareness Month, Cell Phone Courtesy Month, Get Ready for Kindergarten Month, Herbal/Prescription Awareness Month, National Deli Salad Month, National "Doghouse Repairs" Month, National Grilling Month, National Horseradish Month, National Hot Dog Month, National Ice Cream Month, National Make a Difference to Children Month, National Minority Mental Health Awareness Month, National Recreation and Parks Month, National Roadside Traffic Safety Awareness Month, National Vacation Rental Month, National Watermelon Month, Smart Irrigation Month, Women's Motorcycle Month, Worldwide Bereaved Parents Awareness Month

WEEK-LONG HOLIDAYS

Jul 1 – 7 Be Nice to Jersey Week

Jul 7 – 13 Sports Cliché Week

Jul 7 – 14 Spain: Running of the Bulls

Jul 8 – 14 National Farrier's Week,

Jul 9 – 15 Nude Recreation Week

Jul 15 – 21 Captive Nations Week

Jul 18 – 25 Restless Leg Syndrome (RLS) Education and Awareness Week

Jul 19 – 22 Comic–Con International

Jul 21 – 29 National Moth Week

Jul 25 – Aug 5 Ohio State Fair

Jul 25 – 29 Oregon Brewers Festival

Jul 27 – Aug 5 Bangor State Fair

Jul 29 – Aug 4 Single Working Women's Week

Jul 31 – Aug 1 Moby Dick Marathon

DAILY HOLIDAYS

1. Canada: Canada Day, China: Half-year Day, Ducktona 500, *IRS Day (1862), *First Photographs Used in Newspaper Report (1848), *First Scheduled Television Broadcast (1941), Postage Stamp Day, Resolution Renewal Day, *Zip Code Day, Zoo Day

2. Amelia Earhart Disappears (1937), Caribbean Day or Caricom Day, *Civil Rights Day, *Constitution Day (USA), Declaration of Independence Resolution (1776), First Solo Round-the-World Balloon Flight (2002), Halfway Point of 2018

3. Air-conditioning Appreciation Days, Belarus: Independence Day, *Canada: Québec Founded, *Compliment Your Mirror Day, *Stay Out of the Sun Day, Zambia: Unity Day

4. *Anne Landers (100th Anniversary), Declaration of Independence Signing (1776), *Fourth of July or Independence Day, *Independence-from–Meat Day, *Lou Gehrig Day (1939)

5. Algeria: Independence Day, *Bikini Day, *National Labor Relations Day, Venezuela: Independence Day

6. Comoros: Independence Day, Earth at Aphelion Day, First Airship Crossing of the Atlantic (1919), Name That Tune Day, *Rabies Inoculation Day, Republican Party Day, *Take Your Webmaster to Lunch Day

7. *Bonza Bottler Day™, *Father–Daughter Take a Walk Together Day, Japan: Tanabata (Star Festival), Solomon Islands: Independence Day, *Tell the Truth Day

8. Aspinwall Crosses US on Horseback (1911), *SCUD Day (Savor the Comic, Unplug the Drama), Stone House Day

9. Argentina: Independence Day, First Open-Heart Surgery Day (125th Anniversary), International Town Criers Day, South Sudan: Independence Day

10. Bahamas: Independence Day, *Clerihew Day, *Don't Step On a Bee Day, Martyrdom of the Bab

11. Bowdler's Day, *Day of the Five Billion, Make Your Own Sundae Day, *United Nations: World Population Day

12. Family Feud Day (1976), Kiribati: Independence Day, Night of Nights, Northern Ireland: Orangemen's Day, São Tomé and Príncipe: Independence Day

13. *Embrace Your Geekness Day, *Gruntled Workers Day, "Live Aid" Day, National Beef Tallow Day, National Motorcycle Day, World Cup Day (1930)

14. Bald is In Day, Carver Day, Children's Party at Green Animals Day, England: Birmingham Riots Day (1791), France: Night Watch (Bastille Day), Stone House Day

15. Canada: *Saint Swithin's Day, Japan: Bon Odori (Feast of Lanterns), National Ice Cream Day, *Rembrandt Day

16. Atomic Bomb Test Day, Japan: Marine Day (Third Monday in July), National Get Out of the Doghouse Day

17. Astor Day, Disneyland Opened (1955), Minimum Legal Drinking Age at 21 Day, Puerto Rico: Muñoz–Rivera Day, "Wrong Way" Corrigan Day (1938)

18. Mandela Day, Red Skelton Day (1913), Take Your Poet to Work Day, United Nations: Nelson Mandela International Day

19. *Art Linkletter (1912), Elvis Presley First Single Day, Get to Know Your Customers Day (third Thursday of each quarter is set aside to get to know your customers even better), Saint Vincent de Paul Day

20. Columbia: Independence Day, Riot Act Day, *Special Olympics Day

21. Belgium: Independence Day, *Hemingway Day (1899), Lowest Recorded Temperature Day, National Bridal Sale Day, National Woodie Wagon Day, No Pet Store Puppies Day, Toss Away the "Could Haves" and "Should Haves" Day

22. Auntie's Day, *Pied Piper Day, *Rat–catchers Day, *Spooner's (Spoonerism) Day

23. Egypt: Revolution Day, *Hot Enough for Ya Day, Japan: Soma No Umaoi (Wild Horse Chasing)

24. Amelia Earhart Day, *Cousins Day, *National Drive-Thru Day, *National Tell an Old Joke Day, Pioneer Day

25. First Airplane Crossing of English Channel (1909), Spain: Saint James Day, *Test–Tube Baby Day (1978)

26. Americans with Disabilities Day, Armed Forces Unified (1947), Cuba: National Day (1953), Curaçao Day, *Esperanto Book Day, *George Bernard Shaw (1856), Liberia and Maldives: Independence Day, *US Army Desegregation Day (1944)

27. *Atlantic Telegraph Day, *Insulin Isolated Day (1921), *National Korean War Veterans Armistice Day, *Take Your Houseplant for a Walk Day, *Walk on Stilts Day

28. Beatrix Potter Day, National Day of the Cowboy, Peru: Independence Day, Singing Telegram Day (1933), World Hepatitis Day, World War I Begins (1914)

29. Don't Step On a Bee Day, Lord of the Rings Day, *NASA (1958), *Rain Day, Spain: Festival of Near Death Experiences

30. Elvis Presley's First Concert (1954), *Emily Brontë (200th Anniversary), Henry Ford Day, National Chicken and Waffles Day, *Paperback Books (1935), United Nations: International Day of Friendship, United Nations: World Day Against Trafficking in Persons, Vanuatu: Independence Day

31. *US Patent Office Opened (1790)

HOLIDAY MARKETING IDEAS FOR JULY

Get Ready for Kindergarten Month —This month we welcome a new generation of children to the wonders of the world through education. Nevertheless, there are many parents who can't afford to equip their children with the tools they need to succeed. This is where we come in. Business owners from all walks of life and careers can make a difference with just a small amount of time and money. Form a group of caring business owners in your community and host events throughout the month that will supply the needs of these children who would otherwise not have the resources they need to start their education on an even keel with their classmates.

In my hometown we have two programs called, "Clothes for Kids" and "Stuff the Bus". In the churches and businesses in the area we have clothing drives that supply the underwear and outerwear for underprivileged children during one and the paper, pencils, and other items that are a necessity during the latter. I suggest you ask your local school for a list of items that their children need. They will be more than willing to share that information with you.

Once you have your plan in place be sure to let the media know what you are doing. Send out a press release to all your local papers and radio stations. When you take the time to do so, your message will reach a larger audience and the children's lives will be greatly enhanced.

Jul 1 Zip Code Day — Today we celebrate the first use of zip codes in the U.S. These little numbers at the end of an address speed up the sorting and delivery of our mail and it is hard to remember a time when we didn't have and use them. As we focus on this holiday at the beginning of the summer months, the obvious thing to do is to send out letters or cards wishing your customers and friends a Happy Zip Code Day.

But, don't stop there! Considering the speed and delivery aspect, why not think of ways you can help others speed up their success? What do you do or sell that could make their lives easier? You don't have to just have a sale. Make today's endeavor a fun and informative event or just post social media posts and graphics sharing tips and advice. Don't forget to check the appendix for your new Social Media Images Guidelines.

Jul 3 Compliment Your Mirror Day — Today is a day to encourage self-acceptance and to acknowledge that you are beautiful/handsome, smart, and strong. I encourage you to make good use of this weird & wacky holiday by helping others see the value in themselves. Beauty care reps, color and speaking coaches, writing instruction classes, and anyone else who helps others be their very best are all business owners who have service and product businesses that make us all better at who we are and what we do. Just a bit of trivia here. Did you know that the first mirrors were not made of glass and only the elite could afford them?

Of course, a card or social media post will work just fine if you can't wrap your mind around any other way to promote your business today. I have designed a simple graphic you can use which you will find in the appendix to make it easy peesy.

Jul 21 – 29 National Moth Week — Moths are not the most beloved insect in the world, but they do have their place. There is even a website at NationalMothWeek.org for this underappreciated

species. While most moths fly at night there are a few that do so during the daylight hours. And another little-known fact is that there are nearly1five times more species of moths than there are of butterflies, or so their website touts, and some are as large as your hand!

Now let's think about what moths do and how we can use this holiday to market our businesses. Moths are important pollinators. So, one way you could market your business is by 'pollinating' the business community with your knowledge. Share from your vast experience in an event or post tweets and tips on your social media channels. In the sample resources you will find a Facebook image you are welcome to brand and share. Regardless of what you do this week you can always wish those you come in contact with a very prosperous National Moth Week. And be sure to check out the 2018 Social Media Image Sizes Guide in the appendix to keep up to date with the new sizes you should be using for all your graphics.

AUGUST

MONTH-LONG HOLIDAYS

Aug 3 – 27 Scotland: Edinburgh International Festival
Aug 25 – Oct 21 Maryland Renaissance Festival
Aug 31 – Sep 23 Washington State Fair

American Adventures Month, Black Business Month, Boomers Making a Difference Month, Children's Eye Health and Safety Month, Children's Vision and Learning Month, International Pirate Month, National Immunization Awareness Month, National Spinal Muscular Atrophy Awareness Month, Read-A-Romance Month, Shop On-line for Groceries Month, What Will Be Your Legacy Month

WEEK-LONG HOLIDAYS

Aug 1 – 7 International Clown Week (First full week), National Minority Donor Awareness Week, World Breastfeeding Week

Aug 1 – 9 International Congress of Mathematicians 2018

Aug 2 – 12 Wisconsin State Fair

Aug 3 – 12 New Jersey State Fair/Sussex County Farm and Horse Show

Aug 3 – 13 Wales: National Eisteddfod of Wales

Aug 3 – 19 Indiana State Fair

Aug 4 – 11 England: Cowes Week

Aug 5 – 11 National Exercise with Your Child Week

Aug 6 – 10 Exhibitor Appreciation Week, Psychic Week

Aug 9 – 19 Illinois State Fair (tentative), Iowa State Fair, Missouri State Fair

Aug 9 – 12 National Hobo Days

Aug 9 – 13 Perseid Meteor Showers

Aug 9 – 18 Skowhegan State Fair, West Virginia State Fair

Aug 11 – 18 Beatles' National Apple Week, Wyoming State Fair and Rodeo

Aug 11 – 19 Elvis Week

Aug 12 – 18 Assistance Dog Week

Aug 14 – 18 Vermont State Fair, World's Fair of Money

Aug 15 – 17 Mae West Birthday Gala

Aug 15 – 21 National Aviation Week

Aug 16 – 26 Kentucky State Fair (with World's Championship Horse Show), Little League Baseball® World Series

Aug 17 – 26 Western Idaho State Fair

Aug 18 – Sep 2 Asian Games 2018

Aug 18 – Sep 23 Pennsylvania Renaissance Faire

Aug 22 – Sep 3 New York State Fair

Aug 23 – Sep 3 Alaska State Fair, Maryland State Fair, Minnesota State Fair,

Aug 23 – 26 Hotter 'n Hell Hundred Bike Race

Aug 24 – 30 International Federation of Library Association's Annual Conference

Aug 24 – Sep 3 Colorado State Fair, Nebraska State Fair, Oregon State Fair

Aug 25 – 31 Be Kind to Humankind Week

Aug 27 – Sep 2 National Old-Time Music Festival and Expo

Aug 30 – Sep 4 South Dakota State Fair

Aug 30 – Sep 3 Louisiana Shrimp and Petroleum Festival and Fair

Aug 31 – Sep 3 Odyssey — A Greek Festival, Payson Golden Onion Days

Aug 31 – Sep 8 Eastern Idaho State Fair, Hog Capital of the World Festival

DAILY HOLIDAYS

1. Benin: Independence Day, Emancipation of 500 Day, *Girlfriend's Day, *Lughnasadh, *Respect for Parents Day, Rounds Resounding Day, *Spiderman Day, Switzerland: Confederation Day, United Kingdom: Minden Day, *US Census Day, *US Customs Day, Word Lung Cancer Day, *World Wide Web or Internaut Day (1990)

2. Costa Rica: Feast of Our Lady of Angels, *Declaration of Independence: Official Signing (1776)

3. Braham Pie Day, Columbus Sails for the New World (1492), Niger: Independence Day

4. *Coast Guard Day, * Louis Armstrong Day, National Mustard Day, Queen Elizabeth Day, Single Working Woman's Day

5. American Family Day in Arizona, Croatia: Homeland Thanksgiving Day, Fancy Farm Picnic Day, Sister's Day®

6. Australia: Picnic Day, Bolivia: Independence Day, Colorado Day, Death Penalty Day, *Hiroshima Day, Jamaica: Independence Day, Voting Rights Day (1965)

7. Hatfield-McCoy Feud Eruption Day, *Mata Hari Day (1876), National Lighthouse Day, National Night Out Day, *Particularly Preposterous Packaging Day, *Professional Speakers Day

8. *Bonza Bottler Day™, *Odie Day (1978), *Sneak Some Zucchini onto Your Neighbor's Porch Night, Wear Your Mother's Jewelry Day

9. Japan: Moment of Silence (Bombing of Nagasaki), *Moment of Silence Day, Singapore: National Day, South Africa: National Women's Day, *United Nations: International Day of The World's Indigenous People, *Veep Day

10. Candid Camera Day, National S'mores Day, Nestlé Day (1814), Shop Online for Groceries Day, *Smithsonian Day, World Lion Day

11. *Alex Haley Day (1921), Chadd: Independence Day, Japan: Yama No Hi (Mountain Day), Middle Children's Day, National Garage Sale Day, Saint Clare of Assisi: Feast Day

12. Herbert Hoover Day (Sunday nearest Aug 10th), *Home Sewing Machine Day, *IBM PC Day, Night of the Murdered Poets, *United Nations: International Youth Day, *Vinyl Record Day

13. *Alfred Hitchcock (1899), *Annie Oakley Day (1860), Berlin Wall Erected (1961), Central African Republic: Independence Day, *International Left Hander's Day, Lucy Stone Day (200th Anniversary), Tunisia: Women's Day, Victory Day, *

14. *Navajo Nation: Code Talkers Day, Pakistan: Independence Day, *Social Security Day, V–J Day (1945)

15. *Assumption of the Virgin Mary, *Best Friends Day, *Chauvin Day, Check the Chip Day, India and Korea: Independence Day, *National Relaxation Day, *Panama Canal Day (1914), Transcontinental US Railway Completion (1870), *Woodstock (1969)

16. International Wave at Surveillance Day, *Joe Miller's Joke Day, Klondike Gold Discovery Day, National Roller Coaster Day

17. Balloon Crossing of Atlantic Ocean (1978), China: Double Seven Day, *Clinton's "Meaning of 'Is' Is" Day (1998), *Davy Crockett (1786), Gabon and Indonesia: Independence Day, *Mae West Day (1893)

18. *Bad Poetry Day, *Birth Control Pills Day, International Geocaching Day, International Homeless Animals Day® and Candle-light Vigils, *Mail–Order Catalog Day, National Badge Ribbon Day, Serendipity Day

19. Afghanistan: Independence Day, *Black Cow (Root Beer Float) Day, Don Ho Day (1930), United Nations: World Humanitarian Day, World Photo Day

20. Hungary: Saint Stephen's Day, *Plutonium Day

21. Alexandria Library Sit-in Day, *American Bar Association Day, *Poet's Day, Seminole Tribe Day (1953)

22. *Be an Angel Day, *International Yacht Race Day, *Southern Hemisphere Hoodie-Hoo Day, Vietnam Conflict Begins (1945)

23. First Man-Powered Flight (1977), Gene Kelly (1912), *United Nations: Day for the Remembrance of the Slave Trade and Its Abolition, *Valentino Day

24. *Pluto Demoted Day, Ukraine: Independence Day, *Vesuvius Day, William Wilberforce Day

25. China & Taiwan: Festival of the Hungry Ghosts, Founders Day, International Bat Night, *Kiss-and-Make-Up Day, *National Park Service Day, Uruguay: Independence Day, *Wizard of Oz Day (1939)

26. 2018 Burning Man Day, Baseball Day (First Televised, 1939), *National Dog Day, *Women's Equality Day

27. Moldova: Independence Day, *Mother Teresa Day, *"The Duchess" Who Wasn't Day

28. *March on Washington (1963), *Race Your Mouse Around the Icons Day, *Radio Commercials Day

29. *According to Hoyle Day, *More Herbs, Less Salt Day, Spain: La Tomatina (Tomato Food Fight Festival), United Nations: International Day Against Nuclear Tests

30. Huey P Long Day, United Nations: International Day of Victims of Enforced Disappearances

31. Benton Neighbor Day, Kazakhstan and Kyrgyzstan: Constitution Day and Independence Day, *Love Litigating Lawyers Day, Moldova: National Language Day, Trinidad and Tobago: Independence Day

HOLIDAY MARKETING IDEAS FOR AUGUST

Boomers Making a Difference Month —This month we celebrate those 50+ men and women whom have impacted our lives. They don't have to be celebrities, just someone who has helped shape you. Perhaps it is a special friend or teacher, a mentor or preacher. Regardless of whom they are, if they are of the boomer generation they are worthy of your thanks. Since we have a full month to celebrate these unsung heroes in our lives take the time to let them know with a phone call, or card. Perhaps a gift or flowers would be appropriate.

One sure way to get noticed is to host a writing contest. Have your participants write short stories about why their special boomer should be selected as the boomer of the month. Be sure to get

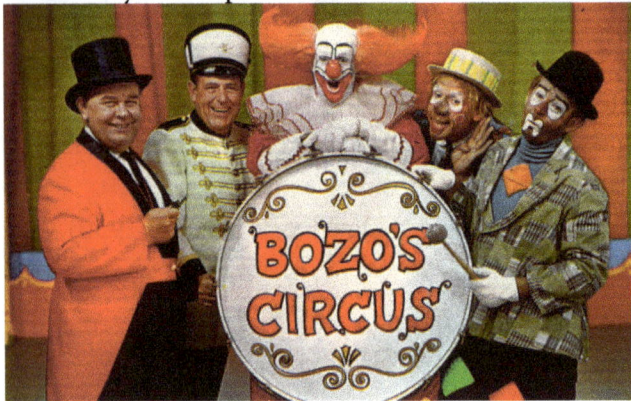

sponsors to donate prizes for the winner. You may want to also have an honorable mention prize and a runner up. You should have a team to help you evaluate; don't try to do it all by yourself. That way nobody can fault your choice and the task of reading all the entries won't rest firmly on your shoulders.

Aug 1 – 7 International Clown Week —How could I possibly bypass this weird & wacky holiday when the mascot of this series is a clown!? This being the 10th Anniversary Edition is all the more reason to feature this holiday. Clowns don't just appear at circus performances, there are rodeo clowns that save lives, and clowns that will visit you at your party or office to make you smile. Some have big shoes while others blow balloons. Even our most beloved clowns such as Red Skelton and Emmett Kelly deserve a mention. And, let us not fail to mention the beloved Bozo the Clown and even Ronald MacDonald.

As you can clearly see, clowns are not something to be afraid of, but rather to heighten your joy. So, while we celebrate International Clown Week let your mirth consume you. Do some clowning around of your own. Find ways to incorporate clowns in the theme of your social media postings. I am sure you will be able to find an appropriate card you can send to brighten someone's day. And to all the clowns in the room I say, have at it today!

Aug 4 Single Working Woman's Day — Talk about hardworking, these women include the single mothers who are among the hardest working of them all. I would venture to say you know at least one, and would quickly agree with me. So, as we acknowledge these tenacious women today our options are just as numerous as they are. Cards and letters thanking them for their dedication and hard work start off the list. Virtual events come in a close second, and social media postings bring up the rear.

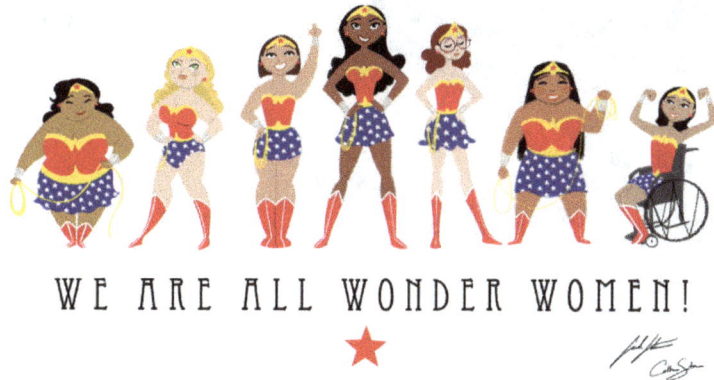

WE ARE ALL WONDER WOMEN!

If you are able to and want to draw even more attention to your business, might I recommend you host a live event in your local area. To make your event different from the norm, consider bringing in business owners who can share "How-Tos" on everything from time-saving meal planning to business and career growth concepts such as time management. If you make Wonder Woman the theme of your event it will add the coup de grâce to your event. The sky's the limit!

Aug 10 Candid Camera Day — Imagine the fun you could have today! Dust off your camera or iPhone and snap a few 'candid' shots to share. Have a Candid Camera Day photo blitz of unsuspecting people in confusing, impossible, embarrassing, ridiculous, and hilarious positions, while their reactions are recorded on a hidden camera. I have always wanted to find a manhole near a stoplight and when a driver tosses something out of their car, pick it up and throw it back into their window! I bet that would have gotten some startling reactions and with a subtle lesson attached to it too. Alternatively, you could have a Candid Camera writing contest. If you can get a sponsor to support your event you might even make the grand prize a camera!

If you would rather not embarrass folks, another idea would be to bring in a photographer to share the tips and tricks to taking a well-thought-out photograph. They might even be willing to take professional shots of all your attendees. Or just for fun you could watch the original Candid Camera show 'Best of Highlights' on YouTube. You'll find the link in the appendix.

Aug 11 National Garage Sale Day — While the first thought is to hold a charity garage sale, might I suggest instead you hold a 'Clean Out Your Closet' event. Speakers who can help in areas such as organizational skills, business marketing or event planning, or even business plan development skills could steer your attendees on the right course. However, if you prefer to simply post on social media, be sure to check out the tips sheet that will help you in the appendix. You can post the image itself or type out the tips to share one-by-one throughout the course of the day.

Aug 25 International Bat Night— Bat Night has taken place every year since 1997 in more than 30 countries. You could share information about the way bats live and their needs with presentations. May I suggest that you work with your local botanical garden or park to sponsor exhibitions and bat walks, offering the opportunity to listen to bat sounds with the support of ultrasound technology? You might even charge a small admission fee to help support your local animal shelter or other organization. Feel free to use the graphic I have redesigned. You'll find it in the appendix.

SEPTEMBER

MONTH-LONG HOLIDAYS

Sep 15 – Oct 15 National Hispanic Heritage Month
Sep 14 – 30 The Big E
Sep 22 – Oct 7 Oktoberfest
Sep 28 – Oct 21 Texas State Fair
Sep 26 – Oct 1 Banned Books Week — Celebrating the Freedom to Read

Atrial Fibrillation Month, Attention Deficit Disorder Month, Be Kind To Editors and Writers Month, Childhood Cancer Awareness Month, Chili: National Month, Fall Hat Month, Great American Low–Cholesterol, Low–fat Pizza Bake Month, Gynecology Cancer Awareness Month, Happy Cat Month, Hunger Action Month, Intergeneration Month, International Women's Friendship Month, Library Card Sign–up Month, National Bake and Decorate Month, National Childhood Obesity Awareness Month, National DNA, Genomics and Stem Cell Education Month, National Head Lice Prevention Month, National Honey Month, National Mushroom Month, National Ovarian Cancer Awareness Month, National Preparedness Month, National Prostate Cancer Awareness Month, National Recovery Month, National Rice Month, National Service Dog Month, National Wilderness Month, One-on–One Month, Ovarian Cancer Awareness Month, Pleasure Your Mate Month, September is Healthy Aging® Month, Shameless Promotion Month, Sports Eye Health and Safety Month, Subliminal Communications Month, Update Your Resume Month, Whole Grains Month, Worldwide Speak Out Month

WEEK-LONG HOLIDAYS

Sep 1 – 7 Brazil: Independence Week, Self-University Week

Sep 2 – 5 Great Fire of London (1666)

Sep 2 – 8 National Waffle Week

Sep 3 – 7 National Payroll Week

Sep 3 – 9 Substitute Teacher Appreciation Week

Sep 4 – 8 Play Days

Sep 6 – 16 New Mexico State Fair, Utah State Fair

Sep 7 – 16 Kansas State Fair, Tennessee State Fair

Sep 8 – 9 Sodbuster Days

Sep 8 – 15 Southeastern Missouri District Fair

Sep 10–15 National Line Dance Week

Sep 13–23 Oklahoma State Fair

Sep 14–15 King Turkey Day

Sep 16–22 Build a Better Image Week, National Farm Safety and Health Week, National Historically Black Colleges and Universities Week (tentative), National Rehabilitation Awareness Celebration Week, National Singles Week, Tolkien Week

Sep 17–23 Constitution Week,

Sep 23–29 Banned Books Week—Celebrating the Freedom to Read, World Reflexology Week

Sep 24–30 International Week of the Deaf

Sep 28–Oct 7 Virginia State Fair

DAILY HOLIDAYS

1. Chicken Boy's Birthday, *Edgar Rice Burroughs (1875) *Emma M. Nutt Day, International Toy Tips Executive Toy Test Day, Orthodox Ecclesiastical New Year, Slovakia: Constitution Day, Titanic Discovery Day, Uzbekistan: Independence Day, WWII Begins (1939)

2. *Bison–Ten Yell Day, Calendar Adjustment Day, US Treasury Department Founded Day, Vietnam: Independence Day, *V–J Day

3. Canada and US: Labor Day (first Monday in September), Mackinac Bridge Walk, Penny Press Day (1833), Qatar: Independence Day

4. Curaçao: Animal's Day, Electric Lights Day, *Newspaper Carrier Day, *Paul Harvey Day

5. Jesse James Day (1847), United Nations: International Day of Charity

6. Baltic States: Independence Day, Jane Addams Day, Swaziland: Independence Day, United Nations: Millennium Summit (1955), Wyatt Earp Day

7. Brazil: Independence Day, Bring Your Manners to Work Day, *Google Commemoration Day (1998), *Grandma Moses Day, National Day of Prayer and Remembrance, *Neither Snow nor Rain Day–Day, Truth or Consequences Day, Queen Elizabeth I Birthday (1533)

8. Huey P. Long Shot Day, Macedonia: Independence Day, National Dog Walker Appreciation Day, Pediatric Hematology/Oncology Nurses Day, Prairie Day, Star Trek Day, Tarzan Day, *United Nations: International Literacy Day

9. *Bonza Bottler Day™, Japan: Chrysanthemum Day, Richmond's Outlaw Days, National Grandparents' Day, Rosh Hashanah (begins at sundown), Tajikistan: Independence Day, *Wonderful Weirdos Day

10. National Boss/Employee Exchange Day, Swap Ideas Day, World Suicide Prevention Day

11. *Attack on America Day, Ethiopia: New Year's Day, *Food Stamps Day, Islamic New Year, *Patriot Day and National Day of Service and Remembrance

12. Defenders Day, United Nations: Day for South-South Cooperation

13. Kids Take Over the Kitchen Day, *National Celiac Awareness Day, Roald Dahl Day, Scooby Doo Day

14. *Solo Transatlantic Balloon Crossing (1984)

15. *Agatha Christie Day, Costa Rica and El Salvador: Independence Day, *First National Convention for Blacks (1830), *Greenpeace Day (1971), Guatemala and Honduras: Independence Day, International Coastal Cleanup Day, International Red Panda Day, Locate an Old Friend Day, Nicaragua: Independence Day, *United Nations: International Day of Democracy

16. *Anne Bradstreet Day, Cherokee Strip Day, General Motors Day, *Great Seal of the US (1782), Mayflower Day, Mexico: Independence Day, Papua New Guinea: Independence Day, *United Nations: International Day for the Preservation of the Ozone Layer, World Play-Doh Day

17. *Citizenship Day, *Constitution Day (1787), Japan: Respect for the Aged Day, National Constitution Center Constitution Day, National Football League Formed Day (1920), Quarterly Estimated Federal Income Tax Payers' Due Date (also Jan 15, Apr 16, and June 15, 2018), VFW Ladies Auxiliary Day

18. Chili: Independence Day, IT Professionals Day, National HIV/AIDS and Aging Awareness Day, United Nations: Opening Day of General Assembly, *US Air Force Birthday, *US Capitol Cornerstone Laid, White Woman Made American Indian Chief Day, Yom Kippur (begins at sundown)

19. *"Iceman" Mummy Discovered (1991), *International Talk Like a Pirate Day, National School Backpack Awareness Day, Saint Christopher (Saint Kitts) and Nevis: Independence Day

20. Ashura: Tenth Day, *Billie Jean King Wins Battle of the Sexes (1973), *National Equal Rights Founded (1884)

21. Armenia, Belize and Malta: Independence Day, National POW/MIA Recognition (the third Friday in September), National Surgical Technologists Day, National Tradesmen Day, *United Nations: International Day of Peace

22. Dear Diary Day, *Emancipation Proclamation (1862), Fish Amnesty Day, Hobbit Day, Ice Cream Cone Day, International Day of Radiant Peace, Long Count Day (1927), Mabon (Alban Elfed), Mali: Independence Day, National Centenarian's Day, National Public Lands Day, National Walk 'n' Roll Dog Day, R.E.A.D. in America Day, Remote Employee Appreciation Day, US Postmaster General's Day (1789)

23. Baseball's Greatest Dispute Day, *Celebrate Bisexuality Day, Checkers Day, Innergize Day, *Lewis and Clark Expedition Returns (1806), Planet Neptune Discovery (1846), Sukkot (begins at sundown)

24. Family Day—Be Involved, Stay Involved™ Day, Guinea-Bissau: Independence Day, *National Punctuation Day

25. *First American Newspaper Published (1690), *Greenwich Mean Time Begins (1676), *National One-Hit Wonder Day, Pacific Ocean Discovered (1513)

26. *Johnny Appleseed Day, First Televised Presidential Debate (1960), National Women's Health and Fitness Day

27. *Samuel Adams (1722), *Ancestor Appreciation Day, Remember Me Thursday, Saint Vincent DePaul Feast Day, United Nations: World Maritime Day, *World Tourism Day

28. *Cabrillo Day, Taiwan: Confucius and Teachers' Day, World Rabies Day

29. Michelangelo Antonio (1912), Michaelmas, *National Attend Your Grandchild's Birth Day, National Biscotti Day, National Coffee Day, Scotland Yard Day (1829), Veterans of Foreign Wars Day

30. Botswana: Independence Day, Gold Star Mother's and Family Day (always the last Sunday in September), Gutenberg Bible Published (1452), International Day of the Deaf, International Translation Day

HOLIDAY MARKETING IDEAS FOR SEPTEMBER

Happy Cat Month —Do you know and love a cat? Have you a cat that pulls at your heart strings? This month as we celebrate our feline friends what better way to celebrate than to support your local pet adoption center? Perhaps you might consider volunteering some time or help with a cat friendly drive. If you are looking for a more adventurous marketing idea you might attempt to host an event online or offline with a theme focused on cats. Here's a couple of suggestions for Overcoming CATastrophic Business Challenges, Chasing of Change, Cool Cat Hot Success. I am certain you can c[...] with something just as cat friendly now that your imagin[...] been sparked.

Of course, for the meek at heart there's always cat care guides and tips that you can share on social media or a quick card campaign to your customers and clients. You'll find a Happy Cat Month graphic in the samples appendix.

IT'S SWAP IDEAS DAY!

Sept 4 Electric Lights Day — Think turning the lights on and you'll be well on your way to an illuminating Electric Lights Day. A card or social media campaign are the easiest ways to celebrate today. However, if you really want to brighten your customer and client's day an event is a surefire way to go. Focus on bright ideas to grow your business. Marketing, website design and optimization, public speaking, social media know how, and networking basics are not to be taken lightly. Be sure to check out the event poster in the appendix.

Sept 10 Swap Ideas Day — The word for the day is "mastermind." If you have already been initiated into this club, then you already know how valuable voicing your thoughts can be when working through them. If no, then I recommend that you start one or find a group of likeminded business owners who will commit to sharing and growing with you on a regular basis.

Sept 16 World Play-Doh Day — Tweet away today using the hashtag #NationalPlayDohDay or take it a step further. Don your creativity cap and nab a can or two of Play-Doh from the kids. When you are done take a snap and share it on your social media channels for others to enjoy.

You may want to have a Play-Doh contest with the most original sculpture taking home the trophy. (Of course, the trophy should be sculpted with Play-Doh!) You could also do a fun facts sheet about Play-Doh. For example, did you know that Play-Doh was originally sold as a wallpaper cleaner!? You'll find a list of 10 in the appendix that you can post on social media throughout the day.

Sep 24 National Punctuation Day — Grammar counts, but without punctuation the words would all run together. So, today we hope to put to rest some of the punctuation nightmares all writers and editors face. Did you know there are 15 different punctuation marks? During the course of the day you will want to spend time writing or listening to the advice of an editor or teacher that knows their way around the written word.

Look around you, punctuation and grammar issues are everywhere! Go on a hunt and see how many punctuation errors are lurking around you. You can find them online and offline as well. Then post pictures of the errors you spot on a special page and invite others to join you in your quest to rid the world of punctuation mishaps.

Happy National Punctuation Day!

For a quick peek at some ways to celebrate visit National Punctuation Day's website. You'll find the link in the appendix.

OCTOBER

MONTH-LONG HOLIDAYS

Oct 5 – 28 Arkansas State Fair and Livestock Show (tentative)
Oct 6 – 14 Albuquerque International Balloon Fiesta
Oct 15 – Nov 30 Wishbone for Pets Days
Oct 24 – Nov 11 World Origami Days

Adopt A Shelter Dog Month, American Cheese Month, Antidepressant Death Awareness Month, Breast Cancer Awareness Month, Celiac Disease Awareness Month, Contact Lens Safety Month, Co–op Awareness Month, Domestic Violence Awareness Month, Dyslexia Awareness Month, Emotional Intelligence Month, Gay and Lesbian History Month, German–American Heritage Month, Global Diversity Awareness Month, Go Hog Wild — Eat Country Ham Month, Health Literacy Month, National Arts and Humanities Month, National Audiology Awareness Month, National Breast Cancer Awareness Month, National Bullying Prevention Awareness Month, National Chiropractic Month, National Crime Prevention Month, National Cyber Security Awareness Month, National Dental Hygiene Month, National Depression Education and Awareness Month, National Disability Employment Awareness Month, National Domestic Violence Awareness Month, National Down Syndrome Awareness Month, National "Gain The Inside Advantage" Month, National Kitchen and Bath Month, National Liver Awareness Month, National Medical Librarian Month, National Orthodontic Health Month, National Physical Therapy Month, National Popcorn Poppin' Month, National Reading Group Month, National Roller Skating Month, National Seafood Month, National Spina Bifida Awareness Month, National Stamp Collecting Month, National Stop Bullying Month, National Work and Family Month, Organize Your Medical Information Month, Polish American Heritage Month, Positive Attitude Month, Rett Syndrome Awareness Month, Spinach Lovers Month, Squirrel Awareness and Appreciation Month, Talk About Prescriptions Month, Workplace Politics Awareness Month, World Menopause Month

WEEK-LONG HOLIDAYS

Oct 1 – 5 National Heimlich Heroes Week, National Work from Home Week

Oct 1 – 12 Buenos Aires 2018: Youth Olympic Games

Oct 3 – 14 Mississippi State Fair

Oct 4 – 14 Georgia National Fair

Oct 4 – 10 United Nations: World Space Week

50

Oct 5 – 13 Canada: Kitchener-Waterloo Oktoberfest

Oct 5 – 7 National Storytelling Festival

Oct 7 – 13 Emergency Nurses Week, Fire Prevention Week, Getting the World to Beat a Path to Your Door Week, Mental Illness Awareness Week, Mystery Series Week, National Carry a Tune Week, National Metric Week, Teen Read Week™

Oct 10 – 14 Germany: Frankfurt Book Fair

Oct 10 – 21 South Carolina State Fair

Oct 10 – 17 Take Your Medicine Americans Week

Oct 11 – 21 Arkansas State Fair and Livestock Show (tentative)

Oct 11 – 21 North Carolina State Fair

Oct 12 – 14 Apple Butter Makin' Days, Southern Festival of Books: A Celebration of the Written Word

Oct 14 – 20 Bullying Bystanders Unite Week, Earth Science Week, National Food Bank Week,

Oct 15 – 19 National School Lunch Week, Nuclear Science Week

Oct 15 – 20 Japan: Newspaper Week

Oct 17 – 24 Food and Drug Interaction Education and Awareness Week

Oct 21 – 27 National Character Counts Week, National Chemistry Week, National Forest Products Week, Pastoral Care Week, Rodent Awareness Week

Oct 24 – 27 International Dyslexia Association Reading, Literacy, and Learning Conference

Oct 24 – 30 United Nations: Disarmament Week

Oct 24 – 31 Prescription Errors Education and Awareness Week

Oct 25 – 31 International Magic Week

Oct 25 – Nov 11 Louisiana State Fair

Oct 27 – 28 Alabama Renaissance Faire

Oct 29 – Nov 4 International Games Week

DAILY HOLIDAYS

1. Blue Shirt Day™/World Day of Bullying Prevention™, Child Health Day (always issued for the first Monday in October), Cyberspace Day, Cyprus: Independence Day, *Fire Pup Day, Model-T Day, Nigeria: Independence Day, This is Your Life Day, Tuvalu: Independence Day, *United Nations: International Day of Older Persons, United Nations: World Habitat Day, World Communion Sunday, World Vegetarian Day

2. *Guardian Angels Day, *Groucho Marx (1890), Guinea: Independence Day, *National Custodial Workers Day, *"Peanuts" Debut Day (1950), *Phileas Fogg's Wager Day, United Nations: International Day of Nonviolence, World Day for Farmed Animals

3. Captain Kangaroo Day, Germany: Day of German Unity, Korea: Tangun Day (National Foundation Day), *Mickey Mouse Club Day (1955)

4. *Dick Tracy Day (1931), *Georgian Calendar Adjustment Day, Lesotho: Independence Day, National Ships-In-Bottles Day, Saint Francis of Assisi: Feast Day, *Ten-Four Day, United Nations: National Poetry Day

5. Chic Spy Day™, Kids Music Day, National Diversity Day, *United Nations: World Teachers Day, World Smile Day

6. *American Library Association Founding Day (1876), Ireland: Ivy Day, *Jackie Mayer Rehab Day, *National German-American Day, Yom Kippur War

7. Blessing of the Fishing Fleet, Country Inn, Bed-and-Breakfast Day, National Forgiveness Day, World Communion Sunday

8. *Alvin C. York Day, American Indian Heritage Day (Alabama), Canada: Thanksgiving Day, Columbus Day (Observed and Traditional), Discovery Day in Hawaii, Fiji: Independence Day, *Great Chicago Fire (1871), Japan: Health–Sports Day, National Kick Butt Day, National Pierogy Day, National Salmon Day, Native Americans' Day (South Dakota), Yorktown Victory Day

9. Ada Lovelace Day, International Face Your Fears Day, *Leif Erickson Day, Korea: Hangul (Alphabet Day), Native Americans' Day, Uganda: Independence Day, *United Nations: World Post Day, World Child Development Day

10. *Bonza Bottler Day™, *Double 10 Day, Emergency Nurses Day, Motorsport Memorial Day, National Bring Your Teddy Bear to Work Day, National Stop Bullying Day, National Handbag Day, *Tuxedo Day, *US Naval Academy Day, World Day Against the Death Penalty, *World Mental Health Day

11. *Adding Machine Day, *General Pulaski Memorial Day, *National Coming Out Day, National Depression Screening Day, Southern Food Heritage Day, United Nations: International Day of the Girl Child

12. Bahamas Discovery Day, Columbus Day (Traditional), *Day of the Six–Billion, Equatorial Guinea: Independence Day, Freethought Day, *International Moment of Frustration Scream Day, Mexico: Dia de la Raza, Shemini Atzeret

13. *Leroy Brown Day, Fall Astronomy Day, Monster Myths by Moonlight, *Navy Birthday, United Nations: International Day for Natural Disaster Reduction, Universal Music Day

14. *Be Bald and Be Free Day, Father-Daughter Day, Grandmother's Day in Florida, Samoa and American Samoa: White Sunday, Sound Barrier Broken (1947), Supersonic Skydive Day, (2012)

15. *Blind Americans Equality Day (formerly White Cane Safety Day), First Manned Flight (1783), National Cake Decorating Day, National Grouch Day, National Latino AIDS Awareness Day, United Nations: International Day of Rural Women

16. Dictionary Day, Birth Control Day (1916), Global Cat Day, Million Man March (1995), *National Boss' Day, United Nations: World Food Day

17. 300 Millionth American Born (2006), Black Poetry Day, China: Chung Yeung (Double Nine), Evel Knievel Day, Hagfish Day, Missouri Day, *Mulligan Day, National Fossil Day, National

Playing Card Collection Day, San Francisco 1989 Earthquake (1989), *United Nations: International Day for the Eradication of Poverty

18. Alaska Day, Azerbaijan: Independence Day, Canada: Persons Day, Comic Strip Day, Get Smart About Credit Day, Get to Know Your Customers Day (third Thursday of each quarter is set aside to get to know your customers even better), Saint Luke Feast Day, Water Pollution Control Day, *World Menopause Day

19. Evaluate Your Life Day, LGBT Center Awareness Day, National Mammography Day, Yorktown Day

20. Bridge Day, Dracula Day, Miss America Rose Day, Sweetest Day

21. AIDS Walk Atlanta and 5K Run, *Incandescent Lamp Day,

22. *International Stuttering Awareness Day, New Zealand: Labor Day, Smart is Cool Day, World's End Day, Zambia: Independence Day

23. Hungary: Republic Day (Declares Independence), *IPod Day, National Mole Day, Swallows Depart from San Juan Capistrano,

24. First Barrel Jump over Niagara Falls (1901), United Nations Day, *United Nations: World Development Information Day

25. First Female FBI Agents (1972), Picasso Day, Saint Crispin's Day, Sourest Day, Taiwan: Retrocession Day

26. Austria: National Day, Erie Canal Day, Frankenstein Friday, Gunfight at the O.K. Corral (1881), Mule Day

27. *Cranky Coworkers Day, Make a Difference Day, *Navy Day, Saint Vincent and the Grenadines: Independence Day, United Nations: World Day for Audiovisual Heritage, *Walt Disney Day

28. Czech Republic: Independence Day, European Union: Daylight Savings Time Ends, Greece: Ochi Day, Mother-in-Law Day, Reformation Sunday *Saint Jude's Day, Statue of Liberty Dedication (1886)

29. *internet Created (1969), National Cat Day

30. Checklists Day, *Create A Great Funeral Day, Devil's Night, *Emily Post Day, *Haunted Refrigerator Night, National Candy Corn Day, "War of the Worlds" (1938) World Audio Drama Day

31. *Books for Treats Day, *Halloween, *Magic Day, Mount Rushmore Day, *National Knock–Knock Day, *Reformation Day, Samhain, Trick or Treat or Beggar's Night, United Nations: World Cities Day

HOLIDAY MARKETING IDEAS FOR OCTOBER

National Kitchen and Bath Month —Have you always wanted a do-over for your kitchen or bath? Well, there's no better time than this month to give your room a lift. Whether you clear out the junk and clean out the cabinets or tackle an entire makeover the joy you will feel upon entering the room will be worth it all.

Start with adding a little color by placing a container you pick up from your local thrift shop or garage sale. Then fill it with fresh flowers. Additionally, a few strategically placed scented candles can add an ambiance that might be missing. Imagine taking a bath or cooking a meal with the scents from your candles perfuming the air.

Now let's think about businesses that can benefit from marketing throughout this month. We have, of course, candle reps, renovators, downsizing experts, color coordinators, and cooks and cook book authors. Another group that might consider this a good opportunity to share are stress coaches. Relaxing in the tub with a good book could elevate your mood. So, novelists this could be another reason to get the word out about your book.

As always, a card or social media graphic could also be the perfect solution for you. You'll find a simple graphic in the appendix that you are invited to brand and share.

Oct 1 Cyberspace Day — It still amazes me how the internet has become so much a part of our daily lives. I don't know about you, but I can recall the electric typewriter and the Yellow Pages. So, since this day is in celebration of cyberspace it seems appropriate for us to spend the day on the web in chats and social media outlets. If I can suggest a way to grow your business today I would have to go with shopping events. Gather some of your friends and invite them to gear up for the holidays by buying their gifts early from each other. You might even try putting up a page where all the stores are linked and sponsor the day's activities by hosting it on your website. Or you could have each 'store' put up the list on their sites too so you'll all get even more of a cyber footprint.

For the faint of heart, you will find an image you can brand and share in, you guessed it, the appendix.

Oct 8 Great Chicago Fire Day — Was it really a cow that kicked over the lantern that started this massive fire? We shall never know, but Mrs. O'Leary adamantly denied the rumor. Regardless of the cause this day is a reminder that we should always be prepared for any emergency. Emergency planning could be the theme of the day. Recovery after loss could be a fitting option. Whatever you chose to do, try not

Currier and Ives—Chicago Historical Society (ICHi-23436)

to fan the flames of ignorance by taking to heart every word you hear and read that expounds on theory rather than fact.

Oct 10 National Bring Your Teddy Bear to Work Day — Teddy bears are comforting friends and so today we celebrate their place in our hearts. Of course, you might dress your favorite friend up in their fanciest outfit and take it with you everywhere you go. Then take snaps and post them on social media showing how you celebrated this weird & wacky holiday. Another viable option would be to give a teddy bear to a needy child. If you can find sponsors who could help you purchase a few and take them to an orphanage you are sure to garner the media's attention. Don't just take my word for it, check this out: http://wfla.com/teddy-bear-roundup/.

The easiest thing to do today is use the hashtag #BringYourTeddyBearToWorkAndSchoolDay to post on social media.

Oct 20 Bridge Day — This extreme sports event in Fayette County, West Virginia doesn't have to pass you by. Celebrate right in your own hometown, or even online, as you bring folks together to bridge the gap that is keeping them from the happiness and success they deserve.

We can't always work, so if you are in need of some well-deserved rest you could spend an enjoyable day in nature. Go for a walk in the woods, hike a trail, picnic at a park, or go all out and put on your own festival and celebrate in style.

NOVEMBER

MONTH-LONG HOLIDAYS

Nov 9 Rabi'i: The Month of Migration (begins)
Nov 24 – Dec 2 Mexico: Guadalajara International Book Fair

American Diabetes Month, Aviation History Month, Banana Pudding Lovers Month, Diabetic Eye Disease Month, Lung Cancer Awareness Month, Movember, National Adoption Month, National Alzheimer's Disease Awareness Month, National Diabetes Month, National Epilepsy Awareness Month, National Family Caregivers Month, National Georgia Pecan Month, National Inspirational Role Models Month, National Long-Term Care Awareness Month, National Marrow Awareness Month, National Memoir Writing Month, National Native American Heritage Month, National Novel Writing Month, Peanut Butter Lovers Month, Picture Book Month, PPSI AIDS Awareness Month, Prematurity Awareness Month, Vegan Month, Worldwide Bereaved Siblings Month

WEEK-LONG HOLIDAYS

Nov 5 – 9 National Young Reader's Week

Nov 11 – 17 National Bible Week, Snowcare for Troops Awareness Week

Nov 12 – 16 American Education Week

Nov 12 – 18 National Book Awards Week

Nov 18 – 24 National Family Week, National Game and Puzzle Week™

Nov 19 – 25 Better Conversation Week

Nov 25 – 30 Radiological Society of North America Scientific Assembly and Annual Meetin

DAILY HOLIDAYS

1. *All Hallows or All Saints Day, Antigua and Barbuda: Independence Day, European Union (1993), Extra Mile Day, Hockey Mask Day, Mexico: Day of the Dead, *National Authors' Day, National Cook for Your Pets Day, National Men Make Dinner Day

2. *All Souls Day, Daniel Boone Day, *First Scheduled Radio Broadcast (1920), National Medical Science Liaison Awareness and Appreciation Day, National Traffic Directors Day, United Nations: International Day to End Impunity for Crimes Against Journalists

3. *Cliché Day, Dewey Day, Dominica: Independence Day, *Japan: Culture Day, Micronesia and Panama: Independence Day, National Bison Day, Public Television Day, Sadie Hawkins Day, *Sandwich Day, SOS Day

4. Daylight Saving Time Ends, *King Tut Tomb Discovery (1922), Mischief Night, *National Chicken Lady Day, National Easy Bake Oven Day, UNESCO Day, *Will Rogers (1879), Zero Tasking Day

5. *England: Guy Fawkes Day, Fill Your Staplers Day, Firewood Day, Job Action Day, *Roy Rogers (1911), *Shattered Backboard Day, United Nations: World Tsunami Awareness Day, Vivian Leigh–Scarlett O'Hara Day (1913)

6. General Election Day, Saxophone Day, *United Nations: International Day for Preventing the Exploitation of the Environment in War and Armed Conflict

7. Madam Curie Day, First Black Governor Elected (1989)

8. Abet and Aid Punsters Day, Cook Something Bold and Pungent Day, Return Day, Shakespeare Authorship Mystery Day, *X–ray Day

9. *Berlin Wall Opened (1989), Birth of Bab Day, Cambodia: Independence Day, East Coast Blackout (1965), Germany: Kristallnacht, National Child Safety Council Day, National Donor Sabbath

10. *Area Code Day (1951), Claude Rains Day, Marine Corps Day, Microsoft Windows First Released (1983), Sesame Street Day

11. Angola: Independence Day, *Bonza Bottler Day™, Canada: Remembrance Day, Columbia: Cartagena: Independence Day, Death/Duty Day, England: Remembrance Day, God Bless America Day, Japan: Origami Day, Martinmas, Poland: Independence Day, Sweden: Saint Martin's Day, Switzerland: Martinmas Goose (Martinigians), Veterans Day

12. Mexico: Postman's Day, Veterans Day (Observed), World Pneumonia Day

13. Holland Tunnel Day

14. India: Children's Day, International Girls Day, Loosen Up Lighten Up Day, Moby Dick Day, Claude Monet Day, National Educational Support Professionals Day, *United Nations: World Diabetes Day

15. *America Recycles Day, Belgium: Dynasty Day, George Spelvin Day, Great American Smoke-out (third Thursday), Gypsy Condemnation Order Day (1943), Japan: Shichi–Go–San, *National Bundt (Pan) Day, World Philosophy Day

16. Estonia: Day of National Rebirth, *Lewis and Clark Expedition Reaches Pacific Ocean (1805), Saint Eustatius, Substitute Educators Day, *United Nations: International Day for Tolerance

17. *Homemade Bread Day, National Unfriend Day, PCS Day, Suez Canal Day, World Prematurity Day

18. Alascattalo Day (About Alaska and humor), Latvia: Independence Day, *Married to a Scorpio Support Day, *Mickey Mouse's Birthday (1928), Push Button Phone Day, United Nations: World Day of Remembrance for Road Traffic Victims

19. Belize: Garifuna Day, Cold War Ends (1990), *Dedication Day (1862), Gandhi Day, Garfield Day, *"Have A Bad Day" Day, Puerto Rico: Discovery Day

20. *Bill of Rights Day, Edwin Powell Hubble Day, *Mandelbrot Day (1924), Mexico: Revolution Day, *Name Your PC Day, Transgender Day of Remembrance, *United Nations: African Industrialization Day, United Nations: Universal Children's Day

21. *Sir Samuel Cunard (1787), Germany: Buss Und Bettag, Tie One On Day™, *United Nations: World Television Day, World Hello Day

22. Charles De Gaulle Day 1890), *George Eliot (1819), Humane Society of the US Day (1954), Lebanon: Independence Day, Thanksgiving Day, Turkey–free Thanksgiving Day

23. Billy the Kid Day, Black Friday, Boris Karloff Day, Buy Nothing Day, Family Day in Nevada, Fibonacci Day, Harpo Marx Day, Japan: Labor Thanksgiving Day, National Flossing Day, Native American Heritage Day,

24. Brownielocks Day, Brunette Pride Day, *Celebrate Your Unique Talent Day, *Dale Carnegie (1888), *D.B. Cooper Day, International Aura Awareness Day, Small Business Saturday

25. *Andrew Carnegie (1835), Handel's Messiah Sing-Along, *JFK Day (1960), Saint Catherine's Day, Suriname: Independence Day, United Nations: International Day for the Elimination of Violence Against Women Day

26. Cyber Monday, Charles Schultz (1922), Switzerland: Zibelemarit (Onion Market)

27. Bruce Lee Day, Cider Monday, Face Transplant Day, Giving Tuesday,

28. *Albania: Independence Day (1912), *Lévi–Strauss (1908), Mauritania: Independence Day, Panama: Independence from Spain

29. Alcott Day, *CS Lewis (1898), *Electronic Greetings Day, *United Nations: International Day of Solidarity with the Palestinian People

30. Barbados: Independence Day, *Computer Security Day, Saint Andrew's Day, *Stay Home Because You're Well Day

HOLIDAY MARKETING IDEAS FOR NOVEMBER

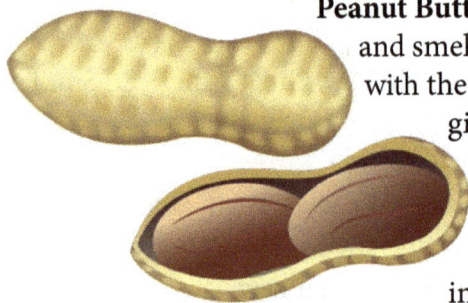

Peanut Butter Lovers Month —While not everyone can savor the taste and smell of fresh roasted and ground peanuts, most of us suffice with the store-bought brands. Then there are those whom have allergies to our beloved spread. Nevertheless, this being the month we celebrate the lowly peanut, we can find ways to market our businesses during the month of November.

My first thought is recipe swaps. If you have the time and inclination you may want to consider planning or sponsoring a peanut recipe cooking marathon. You'll probably want to give a peanut inspired award to the top contenders.

Since some folks can't even be around our beloved peanut, alternatively you could offer peanut allergy awareness information sharing.

Imagine the fun of daily posting peanut facts and quotes. I hear you, where would you begin to find quotes based on peanuts? Lest you forget, one of our past presidents was at one time a

Georgia peanut farmer. I am sure you'll find facts and quotes you can use with a quick internet search. But, to make it easy for you I have compiled a few which you will find in the appendix.

Nov 3 National Bison Day — This animal, also known as the American buffalo, once roamed the grasslands of North America in massive herds, and became nearly extinct by a combination of commercial Bison hunting and slaughter in the 19th century and introduction of bovine diseases from domestic cattle.

Beards for Bison (link in the appendix) encourages us to engage on social media using #NationalBisonDay and through the Beards for Bison campaign, where to snap a photo of themselves wearing a beard (real, or a fake one printed from beardsforbison.org) and post it to social media. Imagine how much fun and laughter will be shared today!

John Calvelli, WCS Executive Vice President of Public Affairs, said: "National Bison Day is a chance to celebrate the ways in which bison represent our national identity, our history, and our culture. The bison is an animal that should inspire all Americans when they see it, and one that should make us feel proud. From its spiritual symbolism to Native Americans, to its history as America's first conservation success story, we commemorate bison this day as an icon that is uniquely American."

Creative Commons 3.0: Photographer: Michael Gäbler

So, enjoy the festivities today and participate on social media for starters and be sure to wish all your customers and clients a very happy National Bison Day. And don't forget to sign the petition to support restoring thousands of wild bison to millions of acres of native prairie habitat on tribal lands. You'll find the link in the Resources section of the appendix.

Nov 14 Loosen Up Lighten Up Day (aka LULU Day) — You know what they say about all work and no play. Well, today we are encouraged to let go and enjoy the chaos that life brings us with a smile. So, set aside your marketing plan — or not — and relax and enjoy your day. Watch a comedy or YouTube cute baby or animal video. These are just a couple of ideas on how you could spend your day. There's link in the links appendix to get you started in celebration of today to get you started.

If you do decide to celebrate while marketing your business, may I recommend you do it with a smile? Keep it simple. Tweet, write an article, hang out on Facebook, or do something drastic like have an online party! You might consider using a 'Letting It Go' theme. Are you a coach or masseur, debt relief counselor, or candle rep? It might be a good time for you to host a 'Stress-Free Zone' event. No matter what you do, make sure it is something you enjoy. We all deserve a break now and again. You'll find a flyer you can use in the sample appendix.

Nov 21 Tie One On Day™ — No, this isn't about getting plastered! Today is the beginning of the baking season and is therefore in reference to donning an apron. You might bake something and wrap it up in an apron and take it to someone in need or who you know would spend Thanksgiving Day alone. If you aren't into baking, you might purchase a baked good instead. Or you could spend the day doing good deeds as a way of giving back to your community.

Setting those ideas aside, you could mix it up with a recipe swap party. After all, every good cook has an eye out for a good recipe, and today they are in dire need. But remember, there's always social media posts, cards, and e-cards that you can send out to your special kitchen crew.

As you can see, I have vectorized the official logo from Tie One On Day's website (the link can be found in the links appendix) and updated it with 2018 date for your convenience and use. You'll find a larger image in the sample appendix. I recommend you visit their website to see other ways to participate and how to wrap your baked good in an apron for delivery.

DECEMBER

MONTH-LONG HOLIDAYS

Dec 2 – Jan2 Netherlands: Midwinter Horn Blowing
Dec 14 – 28 Halcyon Days
Dec 14 – Jan 5, 2018 Christmas Bird Count
Dec 17 – Feb 3, 2018 Take a New Year's Resolution to Stop Smoking (TANYRSS)
Bingo's Birthday Month, Christmas New Orleans Style, National Impaired Driving Prevention Month, National Write a Business Plan Month, Safe Toys and Gifts Month, Worldwide Food Service Safety Month

WEEK-LONG HOLIDAYS

Dec 3 – 7 Cookie Exchange Week, National Older Driver Safety Awareness Week

Dec 3 – 10 Clerc-Gallaudet Week, Chanukah

Dec 7 – 8 Christmas Walk and House Tour

Dec 10 – 17 Human Rights Week

Dec 17 – 23 Saturnalia

Dec 26 – Jan 1, 2017 Kwanzaa

DAILY HOLIDAYS

1. Antarctica Day, *Basketball Day, *Bifocals at the Monitor Liberation Day, Christmas Candle Lightings, *Civil Air Patrol Day, Day With(out) Art, Portugal: Independence Day, Rosa Parks Day, *United Nations: World AIDS Day

2. Advent (First Sunday), *Artificial Heart Transplant Day (1967), Chanukah (begins at sundown), England: Walter Plinge Day, *Joseph Bell (1837), *Safety Razor Day, *Special Education Day, United Arab Emirates: Independence Day, *United Nations: International Day for the Abolition of Slavery Day

3. First Heart Transplant (1967), *United Nations: International Day of Persons with Disabilities

4. Mary Celeste Discovery Day, National Grange Day, Saint Barbara's Day, *Samuel Butler (1835)

5. *AFL–CIO Founded (1955), Austria: Krampuslauf, *Bathtub Party Day, "Irrational Exuberance" Day, Montgomery Bus Boycott Remembrance Day, Special Kids Day, *United

Nations: International Volunteer Day for Economic and Social Development, United Nations: World Soil Day, *Walt Disney (1901)

6. Finland: Independence Day, National Christmas Tree Lighting (tentative), *National Miners' Day, *National Pawnbrokers Day, *Saint Nicholas Day

7. Ghana: National Farmers' Day, Iran: Students, *National Fire Safety Council Founding (1979), *National Pearl Harbor Remembrance Day, National Sales Person's Day, *United Nations: International Civil Aviation Day

8. *Eli Whitney (1765), Feast of Immaculate Conception, Gingerbread Decorating Day, Guam: Lady of Camarin Day, Intermediate-Range Nuclear Forces Treaty (INF) Signed (1987), NAFTA Day, National Day of the Horse, National Lard Day, Soviet Union Dissolved (1991)

9. *United Nations: International Anti-Corruption Day

10. *Ada Lovelace (1815), *Dewey Decimal System Day, *Emily Dickinson (1830), *Human Rights Day, James Addams Day, *Nobel Prize Awards Ceremonies, *Thomas Hopkins Gallaudet (1787), *United Nations: Human Rights Day

11. Burkino Faso: Independence Day, Kaleidoscope Day, *UNICEF Birthday, *United Nations: International Mountain Day

12. *Bonza Bottler Day™, Day of Our Lady of Guadalupe, Kenya: Jamhuri Day (Independence Day), Mexico: Guadalupe Day, *Poinsettia Day, *Puerto Rico: Las Mañanitas

13. *New Zealand Discovery (1642), Sweden: Saint Lucia Day

14. *Doolittle Day, Nostradamus (1503), Official Lost and Found Day, South Pole Discovery (1911)

15. *Bill of Rights Day, *Cat Herders Day, Puerto Rico: Navidades

16. Bahrain: Independence Day, *Barbie and Barney Backlash Day, Boston Tea Party Day, *Jane Austen (1775), Kazakhstan: Independence Day, *Ludwig Van Beethoven (1770), Mexico: Posadas, *United Nations: Zionism Day

17. *Azteck Calendar Stone Discovery Day (1790), *Clean Air Day, *Joseph Henry (1797), *Wright Brothers Day

18. Asarah B'Tevet, *Benjamin O Davis, Jr. (1912), *Joseph Grimaldi (1778), Mexico: Feast of Our Lady of Solitude, *United Nations: International Migrants Day

19. Titanic Day

20. Cathode-Ray Tube Day, Montgomery Bus Boycott Ends (1956), *Mudd Day, *United Nations: International Human Solidarity Day

21. Celebrate Short Fiction Day, Benjamin Disraeli Birth (1804), *Crossword Puzzle Day, *Forefathers Day, *Heinrich Böll (1917), *Humbug Day, *Phileas Fogg Win a Wager Day, Pilgrim Landing, Underdog Day, Yalda, Yule

22. Be a Lover of Silence Day, First Gorilla Born in Captivity (1956), *Giacomo Puccini (1858), Oglethorpe Day

23. *Federal Reserve System (1913), First Non-stop Flight Around the World (1987), HumanLight Celebration Day, Japan: Birthday of the Emperor, Metric Conversion Act (1975), *Transistor Day (1947)

24. Austria: "Silent Night, Holy Night", *Christmas Eve, *James Prescott Joule (1818), Libya: Independence Day

25. *A'Phabet Day or No-L-Day, *Christmas Day, Cuba: Christmas Returns, *Clara Barton (1821), Washington Crosses the Delaware (1776)

26. *Bahamas: Junkanoo, Boxing Day, Ireland: Day of the Wren, Luxembourg: Blessing of the Wine, National Candy Cane Day, *National Whiner's Day, Radium Discovery Day, Saint Stephen's Day, Second Day of Christmas, Slovenia: Independence Day, South Africa: Day of Goodwill, *United Nations: Boxing Day

27. "Howdy Doody" Day, *Johannes Kepler (1571), *Louis Pasteur (1822), Saint John

28. Australia: Proclamation Day, *Cinema Day, Endangered Species Day, *Holy Innocents Day or Childermas, *Pledge of Allegiance Day

29. Andrew Johnson Wreath-Laying, No Interruptions Day, Saint Thomas of Canterbury: Feast Day, *Tick Tock Day, *YMCA Day

30. *Falling Needles Family Fest Day, *Rudyard Kipling (1865), USSR DAY (1922)

31. *First Nights, First US Bank Opens (1781), *Japan: Namahage, *Leap Second Adjustment Time Day, *Make Up Your Mind Day, *New Year's Eve, New Year's Banished Words List, No Interruptions Day, Saint Sylvester's Day, Scotland: Hogmany

HOLIDAY MARKETING IDEAS FOR DECEMBER

Dec 4 National Grange Day — Today we celebrate the first organized agricultural movement in the USA. This is a day to commemorate not only the history of your own Grange but the history of Grange itself within your community. We are a community of caring, not only for our resources but for each other. So, you have two really good options. One is to get off your bum and participate by helping your neighbors, or have a bake sale to fundraiser for your local school or homeless shelter. Another would be to recognize the unsung heroes in your hometown like firemen, an outstanding police person, teacher, or civic leader. If you decide to do this, you will want to ask your local community or school to ask their populace to write a brief paragraph or two about their candidate. Then assign a committee to review and recommend the winner. The media love this type of event if you let them know! Furthermore, you don't have to have a dinner to recognize the winner. However, a local restaurant or hotel might help sponsor the event if you ask them. You'll find more information on the *National Grange Association* website. Their link can be found in the resources, as well, for further information.

The very least you can do is to post a simple graphic on your social media channels. You'll find one in the appendix that you are welcome to brand and use as you see fit.

Dec 7 National Sales Person's Day — Today we recognize our helpful sales people who graciously direct us to the items we seek when we are lost in the mire of available merchandise. Even online stores have 'chat' services as they realize just how very important the 'someone to talk to' is to their bottom line.

One of the very best suggestions I have for you to show your appreciation for your favorite business owner or sales person is to send them a referral.

Do you love a product you purchased? Write a review on their website, if you are allowed. If not, send them a note of thanks. Remember, a real card is better than an e-card — if you know whom and to where to address it. I have provided a graphic for you if you merely want to post on your social media channels. You'll find it in the appendix.

If you happen to be out and about take the time to thank your service provider in person. This is sure to make them smile.

Sales & Marketing Management offers some excellent advice on how to be the best sales person you can be. I have copied their advice and placed it in the appendix for your perusal. However, I do suggest you visit their website and perhaps even sign-up for their newsletter. You'll find their website listed in the resources.

Dec 21 Crossword Puzzle Day — It's time to sharpen your pencil and your mind. Today is the perfect day to learn some new words and their definitions. As you think about ways to celebrate while building your business consider a crossword puzzle contest. See who can finish the puzzle of choice in the shortest amount of time. Have your attendees work alone or in pairs. These puzzles are available online, so you can even host your event virtually. You'll find a couple of puzzle sites in the appendix. And the winner gets … a crossword puzzle book / set — if online, a subscription to an online puzzle site.

Another fun thing you could do would be to give words and ask for the definitions or the other way around. Either way could make for a fun and frivolous day. And as always, a simple graphic or social media posts will always suffice.

Dec 29 No Interruptions Day — When you are diligently working on a project and get interrupted you lose not only your concentration but time. When you attempt to get back to what you were doing you find yourself trying to 'get back in the groove.' That can be frustrating, to say the least, and your productivity is affected by the lost time. So, today you should try to focus on what you need to do. Turn off your cell phone, ask your friends and coworkers to hold all calls, or hang a 'Do Not Disturb' door hanger or sign on your office door. You only have a few more

days to prepare for the new year ahead. So, get to it! Time's a wasting. You'll find a blank template and a DND doorhanger in the appendix for your use.

Alternatively, you could go with the flow and make the whole day an interruption. Slip into something comfortable and prop your feet up. Grab a good book, or slip into a bubble bath. Take the day completely off and unplug for the day. Take a friend or family member on an indoor picnic. Keep your mind open and you'll come up with a fun way to spend the day.

If you are up to hosting an event, consider a time or stress management or a business marketing planning and development theme. Even career planning or 'A New Year, A New You!' could draw a crowd. These are just a few that immediately come to mind. I am certain that if you put your thinking cap on you'll end the year with a bang.

Appendix A: SAMPLES

Sample Press Release

FOR IMMEDIATE RELEASE

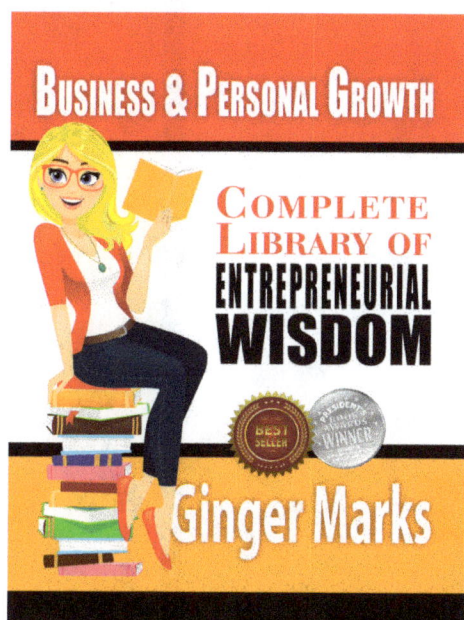

30+ YEAR LOCAL VETERAN BUSINESS OWNER / AUTHOR PARTNERS WITH PNC BANK

CLEARWATER, FL— SEPTEMBER 21, 2014 Local author and publisher, Ginger Marks, partners with Clearwater's PNC Bank to provide insight and advice for prospective, new, and experienced business owners. Ginger will be available to chat and sign copies of her award winning book, Complete Library of Entrepreneurial Wisdom, and PNC Financial experts will be on hand to field your questions and educate you on business financial matters.

Mrs. Marks has spent 30+ years in the Tampa Bay area honing her skill as an entrepreneur. Having owned and operated multiple businesses, including a restaurant and a multi-million dollar surgical clinic, she knows her way around business and how to operate one successfully.

Mrs. Marks states, "Owning a business takes many talents and the determination to succeed. In the course of my business operations I have experienced both the ups and the downs of the financial market. Without the knowledge of how to structure your finances to support your dreams you endanger your success. This is why I have partnered with PNC with the release of this important work."

Event date and location: October 9, 2014 between 5:30 and 6:30 pm at 2498 Gulf-to-Bay Blvd. Books available at your local bookstore and at this event.

# # #

MEDIA CONTACT: Ginger Marks, ginger.marks@documeantdesigns.com 1–727–565–8500.

Frankenstein Day Poster

Customize these designs with your business name and URL. Need help? Contact Ginger for assistance at support@holidaymarketingguide.com or designer@documeantdesigns.com.

Note: If you would like any of the full-size images provided in this book please email me at designer@documeantdesigns.com.

Get Out Your Guitar Day Flyer

[YOUR COMPANY]

WISHING YOU A HAPPY

GET OUT YOUR GUITAR DAY

FEBRUARY 11, 2018

Pangolin Pin & Cards

Illustration & Design by DocUmeant Designs

This pin is 3.5 x 2-inches and can also be printed as a business card if you prefer. Circular logo designed by M. Lombardi for 2015.

Pin

Business Card Size

Business Card Size

Clap4Health Day Flyer

Courtesy of https://Clap4Health.com

CLAPPING CAN CHANGE YOUR LIFE!
Clap4Health!SM Fundraiser

"When you're happy and you know it, clap your hands". Clap Clap!
Created by Shape Up US, a 501c3 non-profit organization — Clap4Health!SM is an activity in which anyone can participate. We clap our hands to show happiness and appreciation. Clapping makes us feel good! But did you know, in conjunction with other types of movement like dance and sports, it can improve motor and spatial skills and enhance emotional, sociological, physiological and cognitive benefits?

Clap4Health!SM Fundraiser, is an innovative solution to keeping fit, active, healthy and happy throughout your life.

Benefits of clapping your hands: Are based on the Acupressure Theory.
"Our body has 340 known pressure points, 28 of which are in our hands".
This is why many children and adults love to clap. It makes you HAPPY!

Fundraiser
Not only does our innovative program keep you fit, active, healthy and happy throughout your life, it can be used as a fundraiser. Host an event designed to get your school/organization moving and to raise much needed funding. Gather pledges for each clap a participant makes during the event or get a flat rate donation for clapping and being creative

Your fundraising efforts support your school/organization by keeping **20% of the proceeds** from your event to be used toward anything you would like

Shape Up Us will match the funds raised and provide teachers across the country with The Hip Hop Healthy Heart Program for Children™, a K-6 grade healthy literacy curriculum.

LET'S CELEBRATE HEALTH TOGETHER! and Clap4Health!

www.Clap4Health.com
Jyl Steinback | 602-996-6300 | Jyl@ShapeUpUs.org

National Umbrella Month Coloring Page

Be sure to add your brand information to the coloring page before you provide it to your contestants.

International Ear Care Day Flyer

INTERNATIONAL EAR CARE DAY

May 3, 2018

EAR CARE FACTS
Proper ear care can avoid hearing loss.

1. How can I keep my ears clean?
A. The ear is a self-cleaning organ and does not require any active cleaning. Cotton buds should not be used for cleaning the ear.

2. I have a habit of cleaning my ear with matchstick. Is it the right thing to do?
A. Do not insert or put anything into the ear. Do not use any oil, sticks, pins etc. because these can lead to infection in the ear.

3. How often should hearing be tested?
A. Anyone regularly exposed to hazardous noise should have an annual hearing test. Also, anyone who notices a change in his/her hearing, or who develops tinnitus, should have his or her ears checked immediately.

4. How long can someone be in a loud noise before it becomes hazardous?
A. The degree of hearing hazard is related to both the level of the noise as well as to the duration of the exposure. It is better to protect against loud noise as soon as one gets exposed to it. Get your ears protected before you enter the loud noise area.

5. How can one tell if a noisy situation is too loud?
A. There are two rules: First, if you have to raise your voice to talk to someone who is an arm's length away, then the noise is likely to be hazardous. Second, if your ears are ringing or sounds seem dull or flat after leaving a noisy place, then you probably were exposed to hazardous noise.

6. Can earplugs reach the eardrum and cause damage to the eardrum?
A. Length of the average ear canal is 24mm. The length of a typical earplug ranges from 12-18 mm. Also the path from the opening of the ear canal to the eardrum is not straight. The irregularity of the canal protects the ear drum from injury.

7. I enjoy listening loud music through ear/headphones. Will it harm my hearing ability?
A. The risk of hearing loss increases as sound is played louder and louder for long durations. It has been shown that listening through ear/headphones at 95% of maximum sound volume for 5 minutes continuously will damage the hearing capacity. Breaks should be taken while listening through ear/headphones.

8. Can our ears get infected by using earplugs?
A. Using earplugs will not cause an infection. Have clean hands when using earplugs that need to be rolled or formed with your fingers.

9. Can certain medicines cause hearing loss?
A. Certain medicines are harmful for ears. They damage the cells situated in the inner ear and lead to nerve hearing loss. Some medicines known to have adverse effects on the ears are gentamycin, streptomycin, frusemide, chloroquine, and aspirin. These medicines must be used only on the advice of a qualified doctor/audiologist.

DO NOT
- Insert anything into your ears
- Use home remedies in your ears
- Listen to loud music

If you have an ear problem seek the help of a qualified physician.

10. What is the cause of itching in the ears?
A. The common causes are fungal infection, allergy, chronic dermatitis of the canal and eczematous otitis externa. After examination suitable ear drops are prescribed.

11. What is the cause of pain in the ear?
A. The pain in the ear can be caused by problems such as impacted wax in the ear, acute infection in the ear canal, acute infection of the eardrum or because of fluid in the middle ear. It is commonly seen in children.

The child should be taken for an ear check-up if the child complains of pain in the ear or hearing loss; you detect discharge from the ear, improper speech development and if the child does not understand properly what you say. Consult your doctor, paediatrician or an ENT specialist urgently.

12. What is the indication of placement of tubes in the eardrums?
A. Many small children need to have tubes placed in their ears because of recurring ear infections. These tubes equalize the pressure between the external and the middle ear and help in the draining out of fluid from the middle ear. Most tubes are automatically extruded after a period of time (6 months to 2 years). If the child still has recurring ear infections, they may have another set of tubes inserted in their eardrums.

[YOUR BUSINESS CONTACT INFO HERE]

Tin Can Phone

You will need:

Two clean soup cans, label removed

String

Hammer & nail

Instructions:

Get a piece of string and two empty cans (preferably soup cans). If you don't have cans or you don't want to work with them, you can also use cups (preferably plastic). Plastic is a little easier to work with than metal. Styrofoam cups do not work well because they are soft and spongy and absorb sound instead of transmitting it. In a pinch, you can use disposable paper cups, but plastic and metal take more wear-and-tear.

Punch a hole at the bottom of each can just small enough for string to fit through. You might need your parents or teacher to help with this. You can make the hole with a hammer and a nail or some other sharp, pointed tool. If you are using plastic cups, you can probably just poke a hole with a push pin or any other sharp point. Make the holes only large enough to put the string through and no larger.

Pass the string through the hole and into the bottom of one can or cup. It might help to push the string through with the end of a paper clip or thread it through with a bit of wire.

Tie a knot in the end of the string that is inside the cup. When you're done, pull the string tight so the knot rests in the bottom of the can. You can tie the string around a little piece of a toothpick if you can't get it to stay with just a knot.

Place the untied end of the string through the bottom of the other can or cup. Tie a knot, as before, and pull the string tight.

Get a partner.

Place the open end of one can over your ear and have your partner speak into the open end of the other can. Make the string as tight as you can. If you've made it correctly, you should hear your friend speak, even if it is a long piece of string. Then, talk while your friend listens.

Gold Star Spouses Pin / Sticker

Gold Star Spouses Day

Recongnizing our military spouses who shared in the ultimate sacrifice.

April 5, 2018

Gold Star Spouses Facebook image

Contact Ginger at support@holidaymarketingguide.com for full-size Facebook image. Customization available.

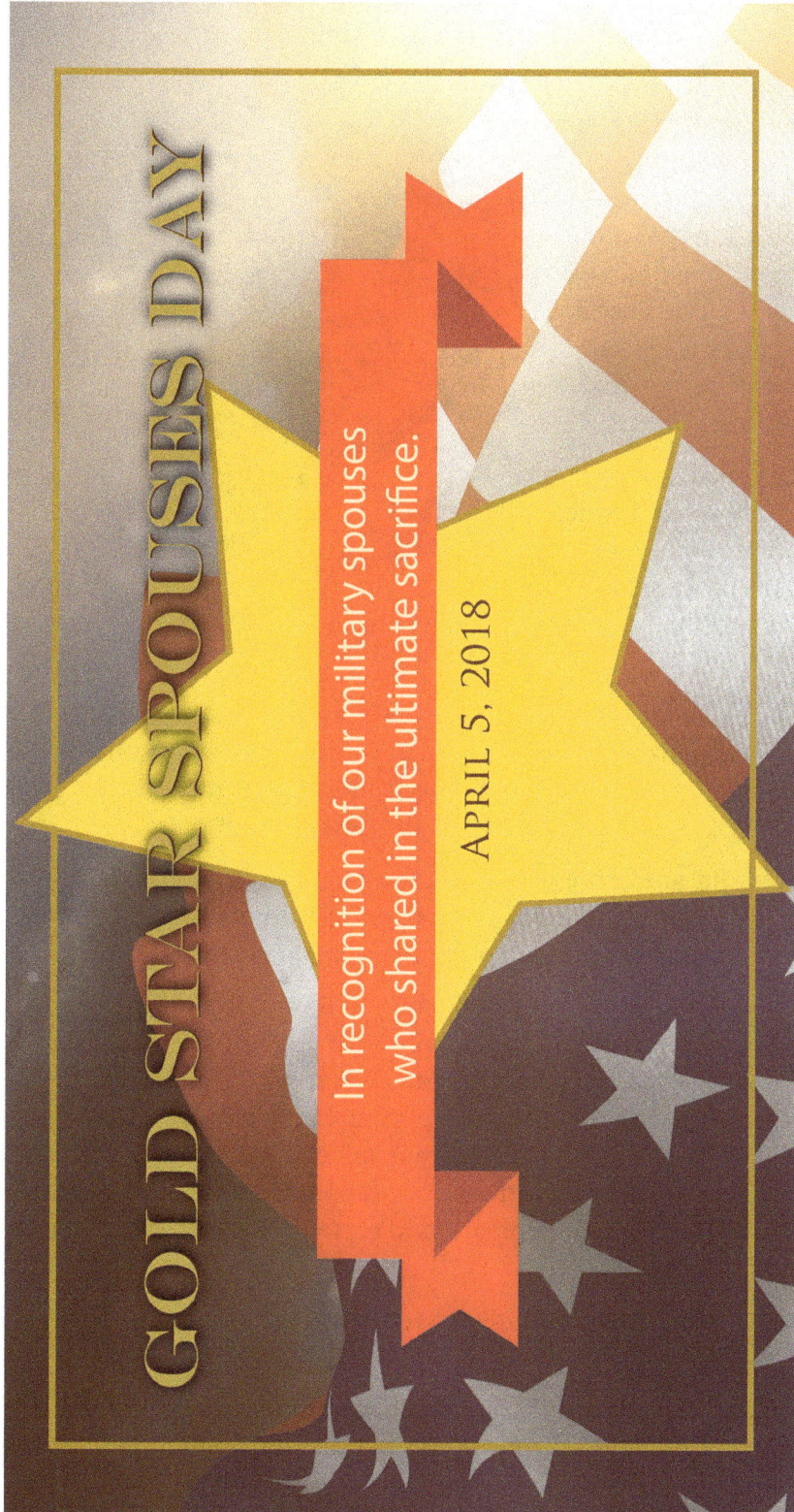

How to Throw a Progressive Dinner Party

How Stuff Works

We know game night is a sure thing. So is girls' night at the city's newest hot spot. But don't discount a dinner party — especially the progressive kind.

This moving feast offers hours of entertainment with a limited amount of prep work. It's a great way to entertain a group of friends or neighbors without shouldering the whole responsibility (or cost) of a multi-course dinner party — all because a progressive dinner party is held at several homes in succession, with a single course served at each one.

Whether you'd like to plan a simple affair or throw an elaborately themed mobile soiree, there are a few basic tenants to follow. The most important? Encourage each host to prepare their course ahead of time so they can join the guests as the party migrates.

A weekend may work best for your progressive party, as a four-course dinner will take nearly four hours. Each course — appetizers, salad/soup, main course, dessert — will last about 45 minutes. Plus, you'll need to include an appropriate time cushion between courses as guests walk (or take a short ride — with designated drivers, please) to the next destination.

If guests must drive from one home to another, the party may take considerably longer — perhaps five or six hours. It will work best if the homes are no more than 15 minutes apart by car. Otherwise, guests will spend the evening driving instead of socializing.

Whether guests ride or walk from home to home, you'll want to designate "people movers" to ensure that guests are subtly corralled and mobilized at appointed times; this will keep the party on track, especially as the evening progresses. Staying on schedule also allows you to predict when you'll arrive at each home, something that's important if any of your guests plan to drop in just for cocktails or dessert. The fluid nature of a progressive dinner party is part of its appeal. Guests aren't locked into an hours-long commitment, but can attend as their schedules permit. And because hosts aren't required to plan, prepare, and serve each course, they're free to party down, too. It's the proverbial win/win.

Taking a progressive dinner party from idea to reality means recruiting the right hosts and nailing a knock-out theme.

Throwing a progressive dinner party is less work than a traditional seated meal, but it still requires some effort — group effort, that is. There will be multiple hosts and homes, so you'll need at least one planning meeting to coordinate the courses and theme.

Recruiting other hosts could be as simple as asking your next-door neighbor to serve cocktails—or as complicated as convincing a casual acquaintance to dish up a main course. If you have a reluctant host, suggest that he or she cater the first course. This way, the host can prepare the appetizers in advance and simply welcome guests as they arrive.

As for the guests, you could stick to your tried-and-true circle of friends or invite a mix of old friends and new acquaintances. For example, you could introduce fellow employees to longstanding friends or welcome a new couple to your neighborhood. While the typical size of a progressive dinner party is six to 10 people, it could easily accommodate dozens of guests, too. If you've invited a crowd, it might work better to serve appetizers en masse at a central location, then break out into smaller groups that travel from home to home round-robin style.

The invitation for a progressive dinner party will be more detailed than most because it needs to include the time each course is expected to begin, as well as the name and address of each host. If guests are driving or walking in unfamiliar territory, you may want to include cell numbers for each host—just in case someone gets turned around. Let guests know they're welcome to come for whichever courses they like, but be prepared to serve everyone every course.

To make your progressive dinner party a more cohesive event, plan it around a theme. For example, a romantic theme makes sense if your party is scheduled mid-February, as does a Cinco de Mayo theme around the fifth of May. Or you could ring in the New Year with your mobile party.

A theme that centers on a geographic location may simplify a few of the planning decisions. If you select Italy as your theme, the wine, food, and decor all seem to fall into place. However, another very real question still remains: What about cost?

A progressive dinner is a great way to party on a budget. Each course could cost as little as $35—or more than $100. The key is to meet with the other hosts and mutually establish a budget to help keep costs in check, which is often the point of hosting a progressive dinner anyway.

Hosts can minimize stress by preparing as much food as possible ahead of time. Many appetizers can be made the day before and assembled just before the party begins. For example, it only takes a couple of minutes to pull a cheese spread (molded into a pleasing shape) from the refrigerator and surround it with crackers. The same goes for premade snacks, such as baby dill pickles wrapped in cream cheese-spread ham and speared with a pretzel stick or toothpick.

Crockpots are a no-fuss way to prep a second-course soup (and keep it warm). You could also whip-up a crockpot-friendly main course, like pulled pork or even rack of lamb—no kidding!

No matter what course you're hosting, keep a few empty containers handy so you can make short work of storing leftovers. If you serve foods on disposable, environmentally conscious bamboo plates—or use recyclable paper or plastic plates and cups—it makes post-party cleanup easier. As you head out of the house for the next course, just rinse the used plates and cups briefly and toss them into a trash bag or bin for sorting later. At least you won't return home to a stack of dirty dishes, right?

With a little planning, even when you're hosting a portion of the party you'll be a guest at the rest. Does this mean you (and other guests) should present gifts to each and every host or hostess? Although etiquette experts are divided on whether this is a necessary nicety or overkill, you could compromise by offering a small sign of your appreciation — like a wine stopper or a homemade treat (like chocolate-pecan toffee, perhaps) — that the hostess can enjoy after the party's over.

Or, you could simply bring a bottle of wine — a libation that's sure to be flowing as the party progresses. After all, the festivities probably launched with a round of cocktails, right? Check out the next page for a few stellar (yet simple) recipes.

No matter which progressive dinner party course you've been charged with coordinating, it should begin something like this: Greet guests as if they are the only people on earth you wish to see at that exact moment in time — and then offer them a drink.

We're not talking complicated mixologist maneuvers here, just immediate access to the libation of their choice. A few moderately priced bottles of wine and a pitcher of signature drinks should do the trick. Just give your custom cocktail a theme-appropriate nickname, and use fresh-squeezed ingredients to give it vibrant color and flavor.

Sangria is simple to make for a crowd. Just combine a bottle of red wine with 1 cup Grand Marnier, 2 cups orange juice, 1 cup fresh lime juice, and 4 tablespoons sugar. Then add about 1 cup each of various sliced fruits: lemons, oranges, and whatever else is in season. Swirl in a couple cinnamon sticks, chill, pour over ice, and voila — a house cocktail. Plus, it can (and should) be made ahead of time so the flavors can meld — just strain out the steeped fruit if it's not as pretty the next day, and/or add a few fresh slices for garnish.

Or whip up a pitcher of skinny margaritas. Bartender Darrell Autrey of Georgia-based Bowties & Shirtsleeves Consulting says that for every four guests, you can combine 1 cup silver tequila, 3/4 cup fresh lime juice and 6 tablespoons agave nectar (which is 40 percent sweeter than sugar) in a large pitcher with ice. To serve, drop thin slices of jalapeno into each glass or garnish with a split pepper.

For a non-alcoholic drink that still packs a visual punch, stir up some ginger-pineapple sparkling punch. Though great on its own, it's delightfully easy to rev up with a splash of gin. If you're serving the dessert course, offer a couple of chilled dessert wines, as well as coffee (Irish cream optional).

Keep white wine bottles and cocktail pitchers nestled in a tub of ice so guests can refill at will; a strategically convenient placement will lend a comfy air of abundance to your party. Plus, when guests can pour their own drinks you can get out from behind the bar and do what you were meant to: Play host — or hostess — during what's sure to be one of the year's most memorable parties.

National Etiquette Week Tips Sheet

National Etiquette Week Tips
May 14–18, 2018

INTRODUCTIONS
Always stand when being introduced.

HAND SHAKE
The higher ranking person should initiate the hand shake. Stand near the person you want to shake hands with. Extend your right hand while looking directly into their eyes and leaning slightly forward. Grasp their hand with a firm, but not too tight, grip and pump it two to three times. Let go and lean back. You can now break eye contact, but keep a smile on your lips.

Conversation
Always speak clearly and consisely. Never ramble or drone on and on. Speak only loud enough that you can be heard. Don't ever try to 'out talk' the other people in the room, especially at dinner meetings.

Respond when appropriate so the speaker knows you are listening.

Interruptions
It is not polite to interrupt. However, occasionally it is necessary to do so in business meetings. Know when it is appropriate and when it is not. Politely wait your turn to speak whenever possible.

Cell Phones
Turn your cell off! Never answer it or look at it during your meeting unless you are an on-call physician. Give your guests the courtesy of your full uninterrupted attention. If you absolutely must take a call, leave the room or table as quietly and quickly as possible.

Name Tags
Wear your name tag on your right at the level of your heart. When shaking hands this allows the other person a chance to glance at your name tag without being overly obvious when they don't know or have forgotten your name.

[Your business info here]

"I Need a Patch for That" Day Patches

Patch design courtesy dedMazay at Alamy

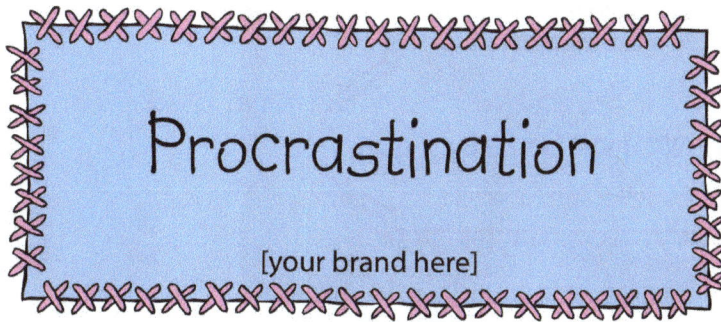

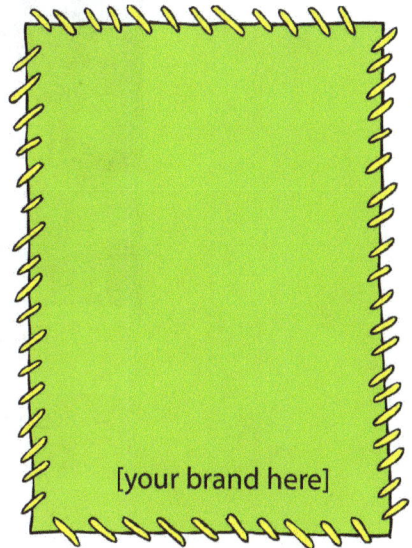

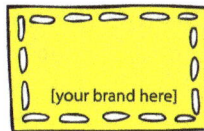

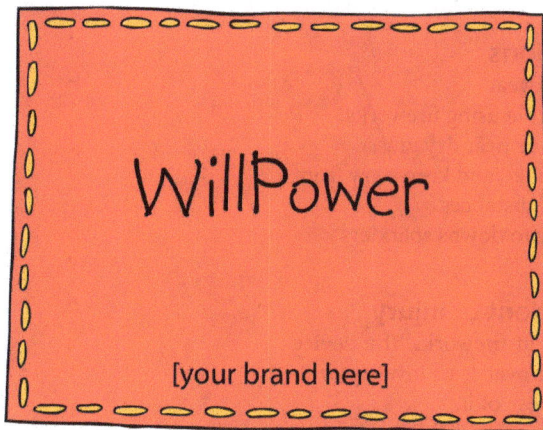

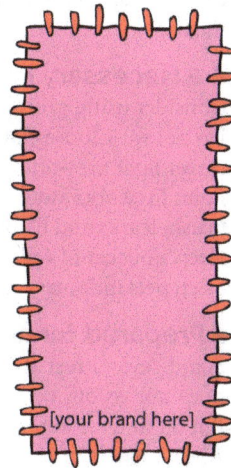

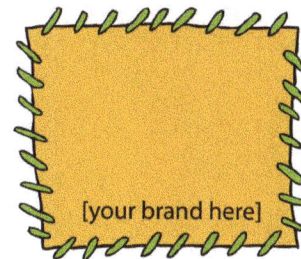

Procrastination

[your brand here]

Eat Less Sugar
[your brand here]

[your brand here]

[your brand here]

WillPower

[your brand here]

[your brand here]

[your brand here]

[your brand here]

Fireworks Safety Rack Card

Basic Fireworks Safety Tips

Fireworks cause thousands of injuries each year. Use these tips and protect your family.

Be Extra Careful With Sparklers

★ Little arms are too short to hold sparklers, which can heat up to 1,200 degrees. How about this? Let your young children use glow sticks instead. They can be just as fun and don't burn at a temperature hot enough to melt glass.
• Closely supervise children around fireworks at all times.

Take Necessary Precautions

★ Consider using protective eye wear
★ Do not wear loose clothing while using fireworks.
★ Never light fireworks indoors or near dry grass.
★ Point fireworks away from homes, and keep away from brush, leaves and flammable substances
★ Keep a bucket of water nearby to downs sparklers
★ Keep pets indoors

Be Prepared for an Accident or Injury

★ Stand several feet away from lit fireworks. If a device does not go off, do not stand over it to investigate it. Put it out with water and dispose of it.
★ Always have a bucket of water and/or a fire extinguisher nearby. Know how to operate the fire extinguisher properly.
★ If a child is injured by fireworks, immediately go to a doctor or hospital. If an eye injury occurs, don't allow your child to touch or rub it, as this may cause even more damage.

[your logo]

[your business info]

Let It Go Day Coin

[Your business info or logo here]

National Handshake Day Brochure

This file is available in PDF. If you wish a copy or need help with branding it with your color theme, information, and logo I would be happy to provide this service to you. All it takes is a quick email to designer@documeantdesigns.com.

NATIONAL HANDSHAKE DAY 6/28/2018

COMPANY NAME

HANDSHAKE TIPS

[Your tagline]

WWW.YOURWEBSITE.COM

STAY CONNECTED

GET IN TOUCH

Follow us on social media and sign up for our [monthly/weekly/daily] newsletter. We value you and your success is our goal.
Twitter:
Facebook:
LinkedIn:

COMPANY NAME

123 Street,
City, State 0000
+12345xxxxxx
+12345xxxxxx
www.yourwebsite.com
you@yourwebsite.com

[Your tagline or mission statement]

OUR SERVICES

Rate nectaquiae. Qui velestiis ipsam, aut vel imaio minum etur?

Os il expelest eos adis pedis estio doluptatibus et et pliae. Me rehende earcid quost, quat occatur? Qui consequissum volor solloribus.

Lorporeium quo cor as nullesc iderum vero blaut late repuditem id evelliquidus vidunti busam, nihitio rporehe nectio modigenia sequi sinci aut fuga. To dellupt aestis ex elendentur?

Orrum consed magniendae nis doluptatiae iur, quist et utatiorae dolorerio. Maion et es volorem fugiaes equibus conseque peribus quibusc ipsust.

Side 1

HANDSHAKE ETIQUETTE

Your handshake speaks volumes. It can make or break a deal, or interview. So extend your hand with confidence and follow these simple tips.

1. STAND UP
Always stand when being introduced.

2. SENIORITY
The higher ranking person should initiate the hand shake.

3. PROXIMITY
Stand near the person you want to shake hands with.

4. POSTURE
Extend your right hand while looking directly into their eyes and leaning slightly forward.

5. THE HANDSHAKE
Grasp their hand with a firm, but not too tight, grip and pump it two to three times.

6. RELEASE
Let go and lean back. You can now break eye contact, but keep a smile on your lips.

3-TYPES OF HANDSAKES

Passive: This type of handshake immediately sends a message that you're uncertain of yourself.

Agressive: This type of handshake sends the message that you are overly-confident or domineering.

Assertive: This type of handshake shows that you are cofident and comfortable in the situation.

HANDSHAKE DON'TS

First impressions last a lifetime, Your handshake should be positive, friendly, warm, welcoming, and the other person should come away having enjoyed the interaction

HAND POSITION
Do not offer just your fingers! Unless appropriate to the event, don't 'fist pump'.

GRIP
Don't offer a limp grip. Show confidence by using a firm but not squeezing grip.

ATTITUDE
Be confident, not overly so. Don't leave them feeling as if they've been mauled or manhandled. Never snatch their hand and squeeze it too hard, pump their arm too vigorously, or grab them by the arm and yank them toward you.

Contrary to popular opinion at no time should you clamp your left hand over their already-captured right hand. This can leave them feeling completely trapped!

HANDSHAKE QUOTE

"You cannot shake hands with a closed fist."

Indiri Ghandi

Side 2

Moth Week Banner

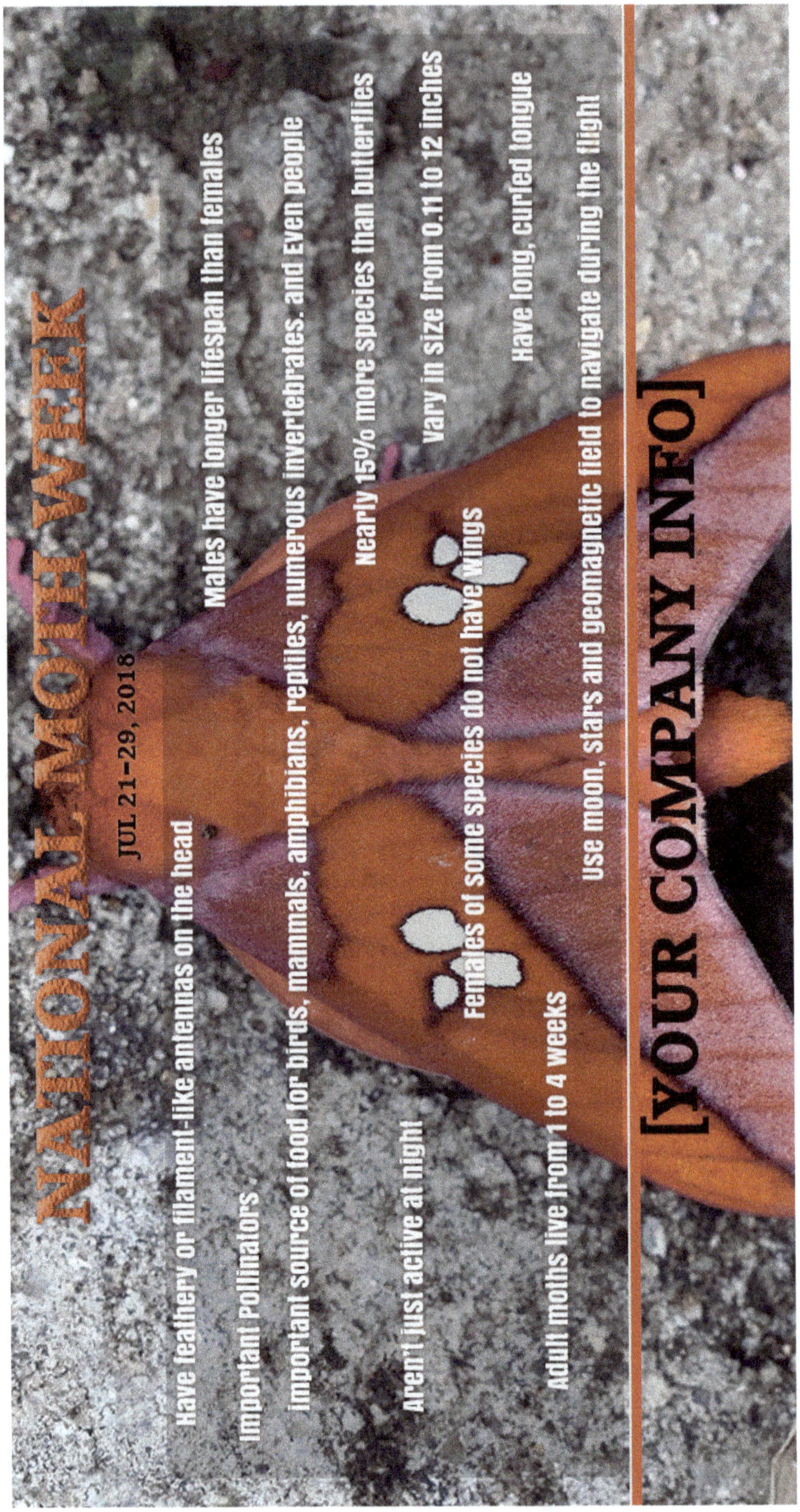

Compliment Your Mirror Day Banner

Rose Graphic Created by Freepik

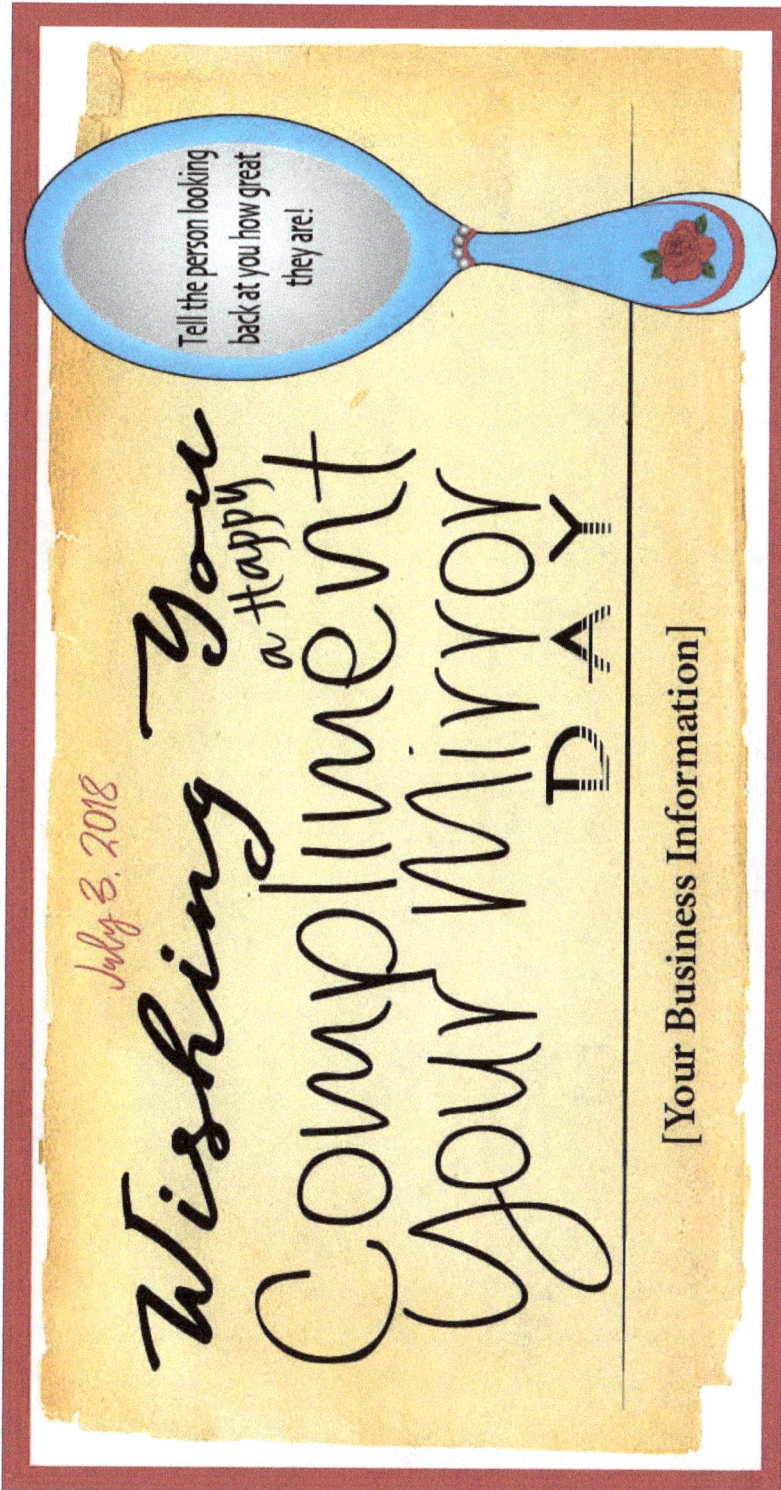

Tell the person looking back at you how great they are!

July 5, 2018

Wishing You a Happy Compliment Your Mirror Day

[Your Business Information]

Garage Sale Tips and Tricks

#10 Garage Sale Tips and Tricks

1. Advertise!

2. Get some ready-made price tags and price your items for their value not your sentimental value.

3. Have plenty of coins and bills to make change throughout the day.

4. Put up signage in heavy traffic areas with the address, date, and time at least a week prior to your event.

5. Use large lettering and black marker on your signage to make it quickly and easily read by drivers.

6. Be courteous and friendly but not overbearing.

7. Display and organize your merchandise to make it attractive to your shoppers. Think like a retail store!

8. Put big-ticket items or eye-candy pieces closest to the street or walkway for maximum visibility.

9. Have a clear walkway so your shoppers don't trip as they are browsing.

10. Be prepared to negotiate a price. You are trying to 'clean out your closets!'

Bonus Tip: Donate the remaining items to your local thriftshop after your event.

[YOUR BUSINESS INFORMATION]

Garage Sale Trail

Saturday 11 August

Tips:

1. Advertise!
2. Get some ready-made price tags and price your items for their value not your sentimental value.
3. Have plenty of coins and bills to make change throughout the day.
4. Put up signage in heavy traffic areas with the address, date, and time at least a week prior to your event.
5. Use large lettering and black marker on your signage to make it quickly and easily read by drivers.
6. Be courteous and friendly but not overbearing.
7. Display and organize your merchandise to make it attractive to your shoppers. Think like a retail store!
8. Put big-ticket items or eye-candy pieces closest to the street or walkway for maximum visibility.
9. Have a clear walkway so your shoppers don't trip as they are browsing.
10. Be prepared to negotiate a price. You are trying to 'clean out your closets!'

Bonus Tip: Donate the remaining items to your local thrift shop after your event.

International Bat Night Graphic

International Bat Night

August 25, 2018

Happy Cat Care Poster

Happy Cat Month
10 Cat Care Tips

1 Some plants can be toxic to cats. Be sure to remove any that might harm them.

2 Cats love to climb, an indoor climbing post placed near a window is ideal.

3 Playtime is essential to a cat. Toys or just a piece of string is all that is required.

4 Cats are neat freaks. So, keep their indoor litterbox fresh and tidy.

5 Collars are a wise investment. If your kitty just happens to dart outside and get lost, their collar can help ensure they will find their way back safely.

6 Veterinary visits are essential to maintain your cat's health and ensure proper vaccines are kept up to date.

7 Feed your cat a nutritionally balanced diet and provide fresh water daily.

8 Grooming your cat may sound silly as they are constantly self-grooming. But, brushing them often can keep the shedding to a minimum and eliminate their propensity for hair balls, while provideing bonding time you'll both enjoy.

9 Fleas and ticks can be a huge problem for cats, especially if you allow them to roam free. Check with your vet about the best ways to treat your feline friend for these pests.

10 Cats usually have their own ideas about how to do things. A positive approach can teach most cats not to scratch the couch, eat plants, or jump up on the kitchen counter. With repeated, gentle, and consistent training, your cat will learn the house rules. Don't ever yell or hit your cat!

Courtesy of: [Your Business Information]

Electric Light Day Event Poster

*Bright Ideas
to Grow Your Business*

Presenter's Name, Subject:, & brief description of what the take-aways are.

Presenter's Name, Subject:, & brief description of what the take-aways are.

Presenter's Name, Subject:, & brief description of what the take-aways are.

sponsors:

Date: Sept 4, 2018

Time: 5 to 7 pm

RSVP: email@domain

Swap Ideas Day Event Flyer

World Play-Doh Day Fun Facts

Courtesy of A Grand Life

1. PLAY-DOH inventor Joe McVicker actually sold it originally as a wallpaper cleaner. The PLAY-DOH compound could remove soot and dirt from walls by simply rolling it across the surface.

2. Over 3 billion PLAY-DOH cans have been sold since 1956. That's enough to reach the moon and back three times!

3. 4 colors started it all: red, blue, yellow, and white. Now the PLAY-DOH brand has over 50 colors!

4. There are 3 main ingredients in PLAY-DOH compound: water, flour, and salt.

5. PLAY-DOH compound was inducted into the National Toy Hall of Fame in 1998.

6. If you made a big ball of all the PLAY-DOH Compound ever created, it would weigh more than 700 million pounds.

7. Urban legend has it that if you took all the PLAY-DOH Compound created since 1956 and put it through the PLAY-DOH FUN FACTORY playset, it would make a snake that would wrap around the world 300 times.

8. Seven million PLAY-DOH FUN FACTORY playsets have been sold since 1999.

9. Did you know that PLAY-DOH cans are made with a tapered edge to easily stack and store empty cans to reuse again?

10. For a long time, Dr. Tien Liu had the awesome title of PLAY-DOH Expert! Liu was the mastermind behind discovering the perfect formula for the original company which was Rainbow Crafts.

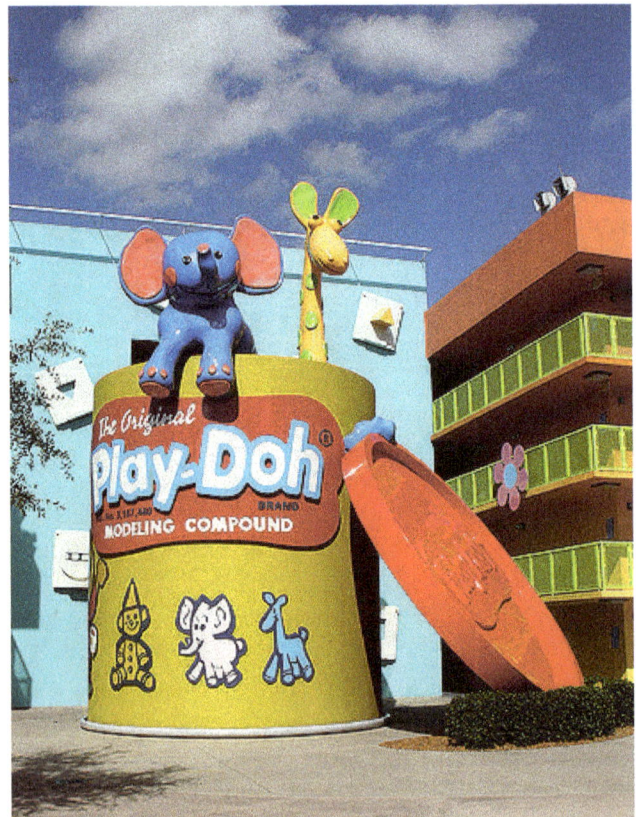

Pop open some cans of PLAY-DOH and get creating to celebrate World PLAY-DOH day! PLAY-DOH invites you to share sculptures of what you imagine life will look like 60 years into the future and beyond. Join in on the fun by sharing your predictions using #PLAYDOH60 and #WORLDPLAYDOHDAY, and by participating in the conversations on Instagram (@PLAY-DOH) and Facebook (Facebook.com/PLAYDOH)!

Kitchen & Bath Month Facebook Image

October is
National
Kitchen &
Bath Month

[your company
info here]

Cyberspace Day Facebook Image

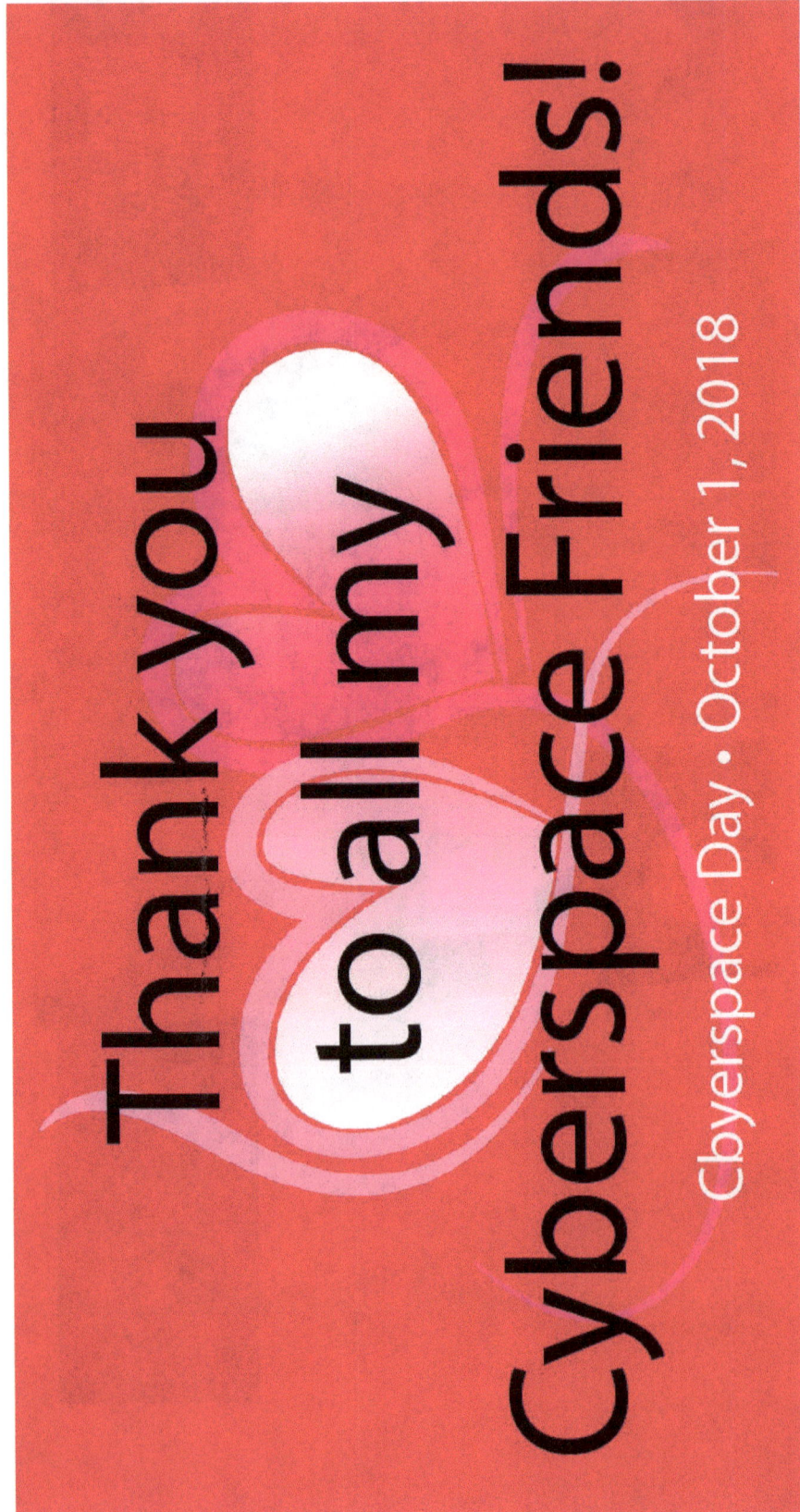

Thank you to all my Cyberspace Friends!

Cbyerspace Day • October 1, 2018

Peanut Quotes and Facts

Quotes:

"Man cannot live by bread alone. He must have peanut butter." —James A. Garfield

"If someone tells you that you are putting too much peanut butter on your bread … stop talking to them. You don't need that kind of negativity in your life." —Unknown

"Peanut butter is the glue that holds my life together." —Unknown

"You can't make everyone happy. You're not a jar of peanut butter." —Unknown

"I almost had an 'I need a guy' moment, but then I was able to get the peanut butter jar open." —Unknown

"Peanut butter is the only reason to buy bread." —Unknown

"There is nothing peanut butter and a spoon can't fix." —Unknown

"If you wait long enough to make dinner, everyone will be happy with a peanut butter sandwich." —Unknown

"It may look like I am deep in thought, but I'm really just thinking about my next peanut butter sandwich." —Unknown

"I don't care what you say, peanut butter is a food group!" — Sally, from Peanuts

"All food starting with a 'P' is comfort food: pasta, potato chips, pretzels, peanut butter, pastrami, pizza, pastry." —Sarah Paretsky

Facts:

Peanut butter is the leading use of peanuts in the USA.

Nearly half of all peanuts in the USA are used in the making of peanut butter.

It takes about 540 peanuts to make a 12-oz jar of peanut butter.

There are enough peanuts in one acre of a peanut farm to make 30,000 peanut butter sandwiches.

About 100 ton of peanuts go into making the 15 million Snicker Bars that are produced by Mars, Inc every day.

Americans eat approximately three pounds of peanut butter per person per year.

About 700 million pounds each year is consumed in the USA. That's enough to coat the floor of the Grand Canyon.

Peanuts are not actually nuts, they are legumes.

The peanut plant originated in South America.

The typical American child will consume 1,500 peanut butter sandwiches by the time they graduate from high school.

Hidden Dangers:

Peanuts are the most common cause of food allergies in children.

More than 2% of the people in the USA have a peanut allergy.

Peanut allergies are the leading cause of anaphylaxis and death related to food allergy in the USA.

Some people outgrow food allergies. For about 80% of people food allergies last a lifetime.

Peanut Butter Recipes

No-Bake Chocolate Oatmeal Cookies

READY IN: 6 mins
YIELD: 24 cookies

INGREDIENTS

1/2 cup butter

1 1/2 cups white sugar

1/2 cup packed brown sugar

1/2 cup milk

4 tablespoons cocoa

1 pinch kosher salt

1/2 cup creamy peanut butter (or chunky but is seems to make a more crumbly, dry cookie)

2 teaspoons vanilla

3 cups dry quick-cooking oats

DIRECTIONS

Add the first six ingredients into a 4-quart sauce pan.

Bring to a rolling boil and hold for 1 minute.

Remove from heat.

Add peanut butter into the hot mixture and stir until melted.

Add in vanilla. (Almond extract is good also, but I only use 1/2 teaspoon almond extract with 1 1/2 teaspoon vanilla extract).

Mix in the dry oats until they are completely coated.

Drop cookies by tablespoonfuls onto wax paper.

Let cool until set.

*Please remember that even if you do follow the recipe exactly, it doesn't always turn out just right. I've had these not set up for me or be hard and dry. But most of the time, the recipe is just right. I adjusted the sugar in the recipe by substituting 1/2 cup of white sugar for 1/2 cup brown sugar, this makes them more moist. I have also found that it makes a difference if you use quick cooking oats or old fashioned. In my experience it takes more old-fashioned oats than quick cooking and I like the texture of the quick cooking better. When you make it a few hundred times like I have you learn a couple of things:) Also, Chunky peanut butter tends to make them more dry and crumbly.

White Chocolate Krispies aka Angel Poo

PREP TIME: 10 mins
TOTAL TIME: 15 mins
SERVINGS: 20

INGREDIENTS

1 lb white chocolate

1 cup Cap'n Crunch Peanut Butter Crunch cereal

1 cup Rice Krispies

3/4 cup dry roasted salted peanut

3/4 cup roasted salted cashews

1 cup white miniature marshmallows

DIRECTIONS

Line a large sheet pan with wax paper; set aside. Cut white chocolate into small chunks, add to a medium pot and cook over medium-low heat, stirring constantly, until completely melted and smooth, 2-3 minutes.

Remove pot from heat, add Cap'N Crunch, Rice Krispies, peanuts, and cashews and stir gently to coat. Set aside to let cool slightly for 2-3 minutes, then stir in marshmallows.

Drop mounds of the chocolate mixture (about 3 tablespoons each) onto the prepared pan, keeping them spaced about 1" apart, to make 3"-wide candies. Set aside in a cool spot until completely set. Serve immediately, or store in an airtight container in a cool spot for up to one week.

Peanut Butter Bars

INGREDIENTS

3 cups rice cereal

1 cup salted peanuts

½ cup sugar

½ cup light corn syrup

½ cup peanut butter

½ tsp vanilla

DIRECTIONS

Mix rice cereal & salted peanuts and set aside.

Combine sugar & corn syrup. Cook stirring constantly Until mixture comes to a full rolling boil. Remove From heat and stir in peanut butter & vanilla.

Immediately pour the syrup over the cereal mixture, stirring to coat. Pat evenly into buttered 8-inch square pan. Cool & cut into bars.

(These are even better if you put a slice of caramel on top and dipped in chocolate)

Decadent Peanut Butter Pie

SERVES 10

Ingredients

1 prepared chocolate graham cracker pie crust

1 egg white, beaten

1 cup Jif Peanut Butter

8 oz. cream cheese (at room temperature)

1/2 cup sugar

2 cups non-dairy whipped topping

For the Topping:

1/4 cup heavy cream

1/2 cup plus 1 tablespoon Smucker's Hot Fudge Topping

2 cups non-dairy whipped topping

2 tablespoons finely chopped dry-roasted peanuts (optional)

Directions

Brush the crust with beaten egg white; bake at 375 degrees F for 5 minutes. Remove crust from oven and set aside to cool.

In a medium bowl, beat together the Jif Peanut Butter, cream cheese, and sugar. Gently fold in the whipped topping, 1/2 cup at a time (a few creamy streaks will remain in the mixture). Spoon mixture into cooled pie shell. Using a spatula, smooth the top and make a 1/2-inch ridge around the edge to keep the topping from sliding off the edge. Refrigerate.

In a microwave-safe bowl, heat the cream on high power for one minute or just until it boils.

Stir the Smucker's Fudge Topping into the cream until it's completely melted. Measure out 1 tablespoon of this mixture and set it aside (not in the refrigerator) for later use. Gently spread the remaining mixture onto the chilled pie. Chill pie again until nearly firm, about one hour.

Spread whipped topping over the top of the chilled pie, covering fudge topping layer. Drizzle with reserved chocolate mixture and sprinkle with peanuts. Chill until serving time.

Reprinted by permission of Jif®. All rights reserved.

Oriental Spicy Noodles
These tasty noodles make a great side dish.
Serves 2-4

Ingredients
2 1/2 teaspoons Ginger, fresh, peeled and minced

1 1/2 teaspoons Garlic, minced

2 teaspoons Scallions, chopped

3 Tablespoons Peanut butter, smooth

2 teaspoons Soy sauce

11/2 teaspoons Chile Paste

1/2 teaspoon Sugar

1 Tablespoon Sesame oil

1/2 Chinese hot mustard

4 Tablespoons Chicken broth

1/2-pound Noodles (oriental, angel hair, linguine, etc.), cooked

Directions
Cook the noodles, drain and allow to cool. Whisk together the remaining ingredients. Toss in the noodles and mix well. Serve at room temperature. Refrigerate any unused portion.

Haystacks
These treats are somewhere between cookies and candy.
Makes about 18

Ingredients
3/4 cup Peanut butter

12 ounces Butterscotch chips

3 ounces Chow Mein noodles (canned)

3/4 cup Walnuts, chopped

Directions
Melt the butterscotch chips in a saucepan over low heat. Stir in the peanut butter and heat until warm. Stir in the nuts and noodles. Drop by the teaspoon full onto parchment or waxed paper. Refrigerate until firm.

Barbecued Banana Split

Kids of all ages love these. They make great leftovers. Stick the barbecued banana, foil and all in the freezer for a delectable frozen indulgence!

Ingredients

3 Ripe bananas

6 Squares of aluminum foil, measuring approximately 8" X 8"

Choose a combination of any or all of the following toppings:

1-1/2 cups chocolate chips

1-1/2 cups M&Ms

1-1/2 cups Reese's Pieces

1-1/2 cups chopped pecans (to make it Southern)

1-1/2 cups peanuts or walnuts

3/4 cup peanut butter

1-1/2 cups coconut

1-1/2 cups mini marshmallows

Lower-fat version:

1-1/2 cups blueberries

1-1/2 cups strawberries

1-1/2 cups papaya

Directions

Place half a banana on each piece of aluminum foil. Slice the banana from end to end, so that it looks like a boat. Place 1/4 cup chocolate chips, marshmallows, M & Ms or your choice of toppings on the banana. Wrap the aluminum foil loosely around the banana.

Place on the barbecue for 3-5 minutes, until the candies and marshmallows have melted. Remove from barbecue. Unwrap and enjoy. Use caution when opening the aluminum foil wrapper, as some steam may escape. Top with whipping cream or ice cream.

Conventional Oven: You can also make barbecued banana splits in a conventional oven. Bake at 400° for 4 minutes.

Loosen Up Lighten Up Flyer

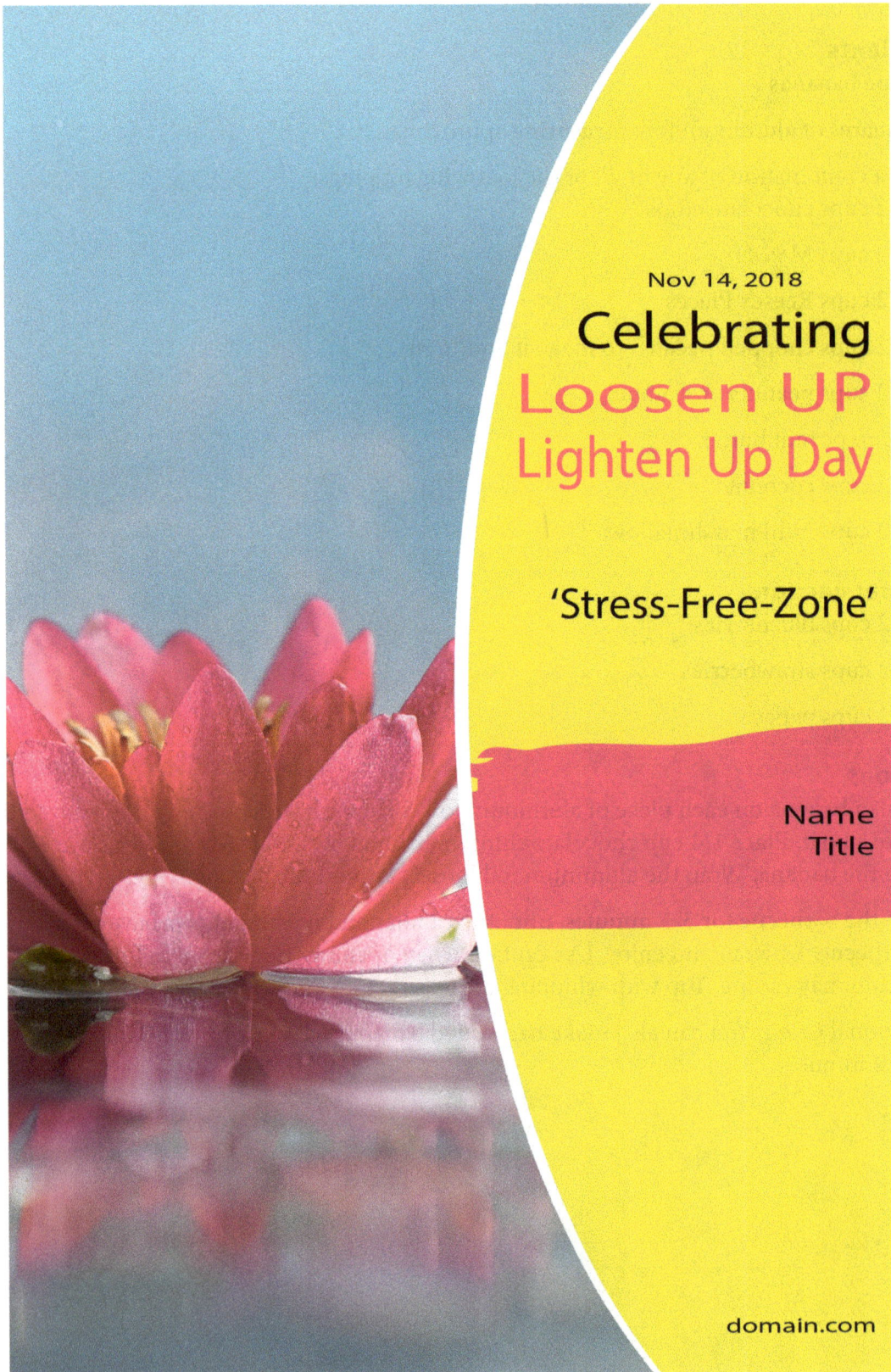

Nov 14, 2018

Celebrating
Loosen UP
Lighten Up Day

'Stress-Free-Zone'

Name
Title

domain.com

Tie One On Day Logo
Courtesy of Apron Memories (Updated for 2018)

National Grange Day Image

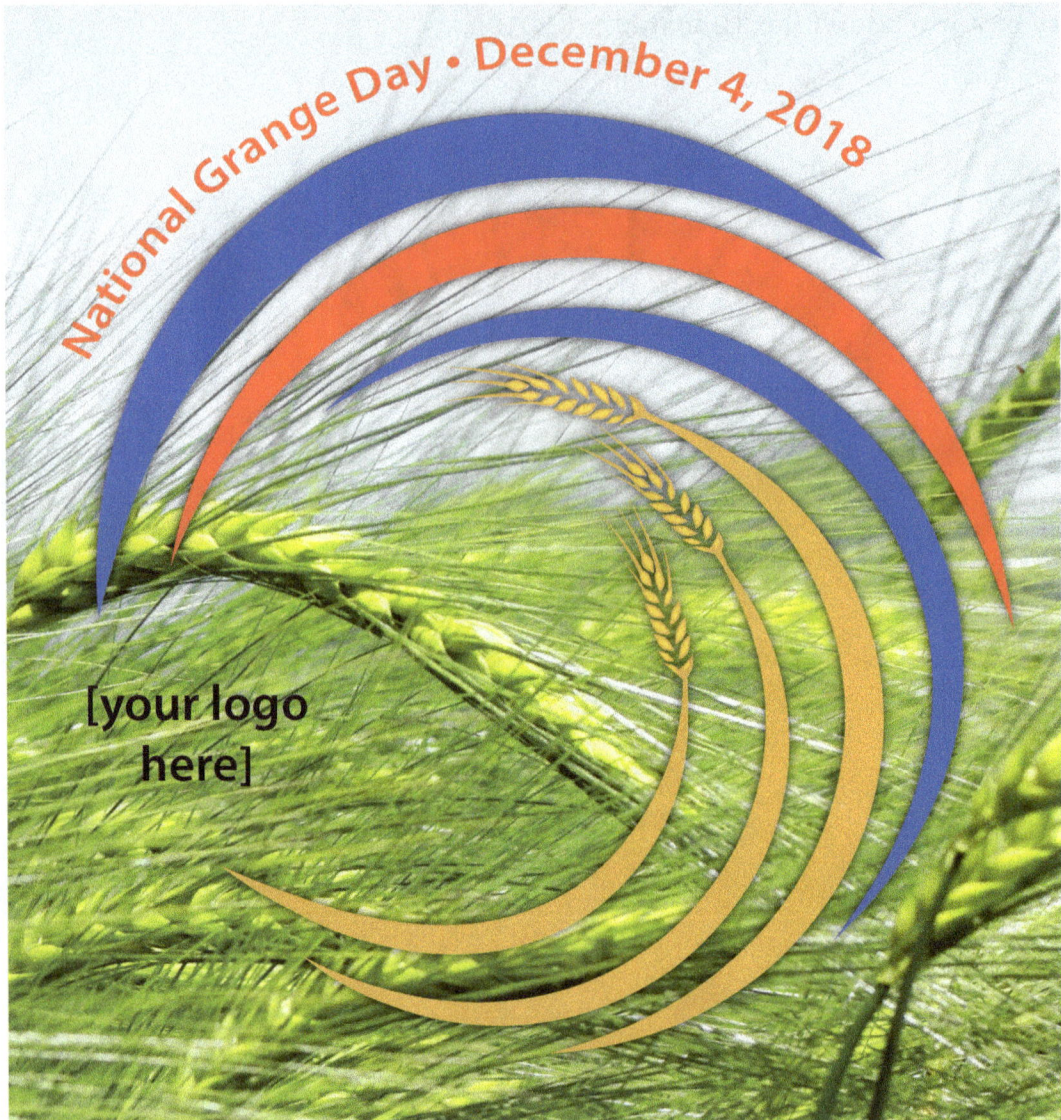

10 Tips for Sales People

Courtesy of Sales & Marketing

National Salesperson Day is the first Friday in March. To honor hard-working sales reps everywhere, Brainshark, Inc., a company delivering content-driven sales enablement solutions that close more deals, has gathered tips from top-performing reps on best practices that can help raise the bar for sales performance and turn "B" and "C" reps into "A" players.

There's no denying that sales is a high-stakes, high-pressure job. Reps today face more complex selling challenges than ever before and are expected to add significant value in conversations with increasingly informed buyers at every stage of the selling process. According to data from the TAS Group, 67 percent of sales professionals do not reach their individual quota.

Reps looking to improve performance and meet their goals should consider the following 10 tips:

1. **Don't stick to the script** — Being professional and staying on message is important, but not if it comes across as stiff and robotic. The best reps have conversations with customers and prospects that balance professionalism with personality. Be yourself and try to find common ground by identifying similar interests, such as sports or humor. The more buyers can identify with you as a genuine person, the more likely they are to buy from you.

2. **Remember to address everyone** — When meeting with prospects, aim to discover the goals and expectations of everyone in the room, not just the people you deem important. You don't know what factors will influence the final decision. The best reps make sure to circle back with everyone — either during or post-meetings — to convey how their solution will address each person's needs.

3. **Determine the next step** — Every conversation or interaction must end with an action. Without that, it's all too easy for the customer or prospect to "go silent." Top reps always get a commitment on next steps in order to keep the conversation going and move the opportunity forward.

4. **Prioritize admin tasks** — Administrative tasks around documenting and reporting every step of the sales cycle are both necessary and time consuming. If you aren't careful, precious selling hours could pass without any real productivity. Make sure to prioritize your time, dedicating off hours — early in the morning or end of the day — to administrative work and keep prime selling hours focused on closing deals.

5. **Pick up the phone, it works** — With email being the primary form of contact for reps these days, the phone seems positively "old school." But the best reps will tell you — pick up the phone and call your prospects and customers. Next to in-person meetings, the phone is still the best way to solicit a response and get feedback or insight into a person's tone and sentiment — which doesn't necessarily come across otherwise. Call on a Friday afternoon when your prospect is likely to be more relaxed, and you'll be surprised at what you can accomplish.

6. **Take good notes** — It is basic advice that's often ignored. Unless you have a photographic memory, you won't remember what was said by whom if you didn't document it. Take the time to write down the important details from your conversations with prospects. The ability to recall those details puts you at a distinct advantage throughout every phase of the sales cycle.

7. **Leave your ego at the door** — Sales reps are highly competitive —it's in your DNA. But to be a top performer, you have to be humble and willing to look at what makes others successful too. Find out what strategies other sales reps are using and then replicate them for yourself. Success is about adapting to what works best, and that means being open to new and alternative approaches.

8. **Do what you say** – Another basic tenet that sets top reps apart: if you say you're going to provide information or look into something, make sure you do it. Your customers and prospects have access to almost everything you do via the internet, so make sure you not only follow through, but that you respond quickly —or they will find someone else to work with. This is a key part of adding value and establishing a positive rapport.

9. **Set daily, achievable goals** — The ups and downs of sales are challenging and even the best sales reps lose more opportunities than they win. To manage the emotional rollercoaster of wins and losses —set daily goals that are tangible and achievable. Creating and reaching these goals will help you stay motivated and focused, and give you a sense of accomplishment at the end of each day.

10. **Don't be afraid to walk away** — You finally got in front of a target prospect and you're doing everything you can to move the process forward. That's exactly what you should do, right? Not necessarily. Reps often spend too much valuable time trying to qualify prospects into an opportunity, rather than qualifying them out. One of the keys to success is knowing when it's just not the right time or fit —so you can focus your energies on other, more fruitful opportunities.

For more information on how to improve sales performance and close more deals, and for additional tips on sales enablement, training and more, visit the Brainshark Ideas Blog at http://www.brainshark.com/ideas-blog.

National Sales Person's Day Banner

THE BEST DARN SALES PERSON EVER

7 DECEMBER 2018

National Sales Person's Day

[YOUR COMPANY INFO]

Do Not Disturb Door Hanger & Template

Door Hanger
3.5 x 8.5

Cut Out

Blank Template

Bleed – To ensure your image fills the entire area extend them to this edge.

Safe zone – No text beyond this line.

Trim – This is the actual cut line.

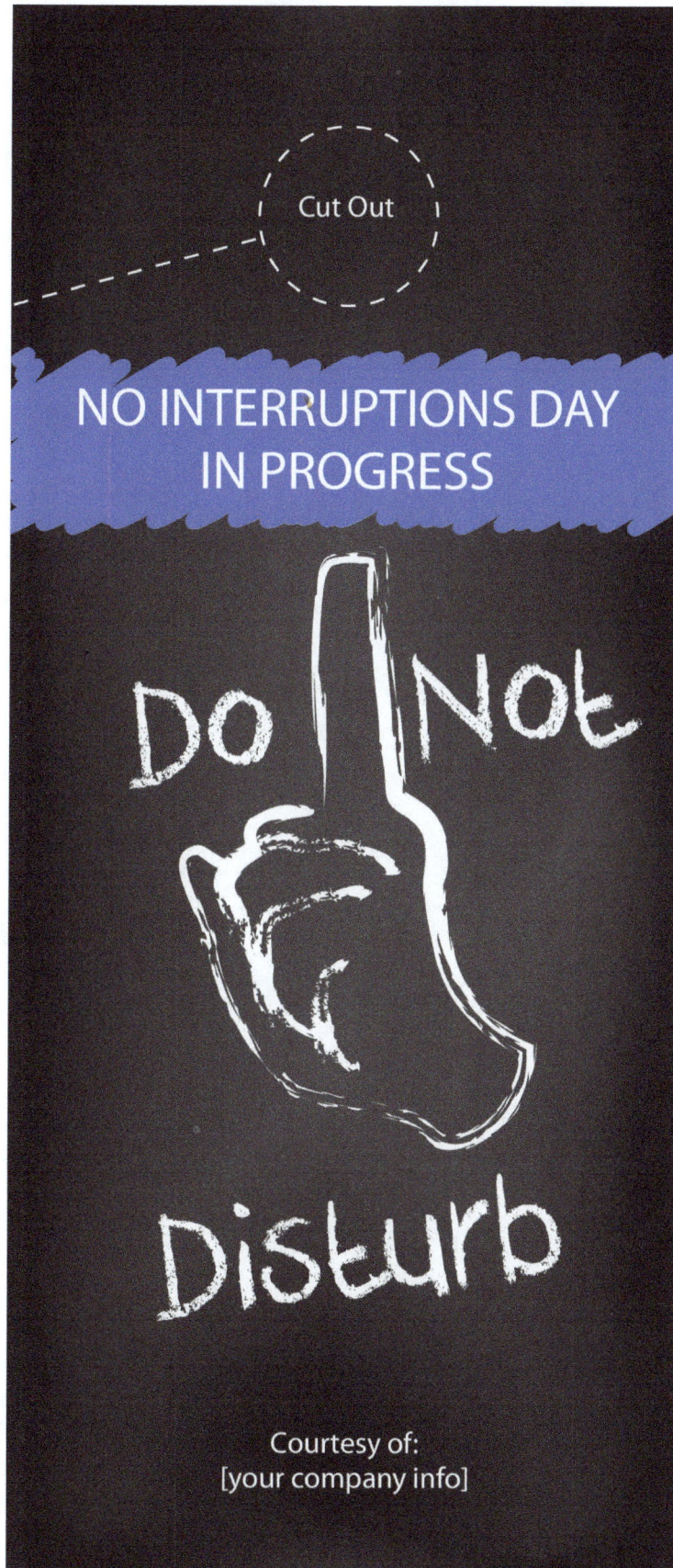

Cut Out

NO INTERRUPTIONS DAY IN PROGRESS

Do Not

Disturb

Courtesy of:
[your company info]

Appendix B: 2018 SOCIAL MEDIA IMAGE SIZE GUIDE

Courtesy of https://makeawebsitehub.com/social-media-image-sizes-cheat-sheet/

All dimensions given in pixels.

Facebook
Cover Photo: 820 x 310
Profile Image: 180 x 180
Shared Image: 1200 x 630
Shared Link: 1200 x 627
Highlighted Image: 1200 x 717
Event Image: 1920 x 1080
Additional image details can be found on MakeaWebsiteHub.com

LinkedIn
Profile Image: 400 x 400
Background Image: 1536 x 768
Standard Logo: 400 x 400
Hero Image: 974 x 330
Square Logo: 60 x 60
Business Banner Image: 646 x 220

YouTube
Channel Profile: 800 x 800
Channel Cover Photo: 2560 x 1440
Video Uploads: 1280 x 720

Instagram
Profile Image: 110 x 110
Photo Thumbnail: 161 x 161
Photo Size: 1080 x 1080
Video Stories: 750 x 1334
Landscape: 1080 x 566
Portrait: 1080 x 1350

Twitter
Header Photo: 1500 x 500
Profile Photo: 400 x 400 (displays at 200 x 200)
In-Stream Photo: 440 x 220

Pinterest

Profile Image: 165 x 165
Board Display: 222 x 150
Pin Sizes: 236 wide (height is scaled)

Tumbler

Profile Image: 128 x 128
Image Posts: 500 x750

Google+

Profile Image: 250 x 250
Cover Image: 1080 x 608
Shared Home Stream Image: 497 x 373
Shared Feed Copy Image: 150 x 150
Shared Video: 494 x 279

Ello

Banner Image: 2560 x 1440
Profile Image: 360 x 360
SnapChat
Geofilter Image: 1080 x 1920

Chinese Social Media

WeChat

Profile Photo: 200 x 200
Article Preview Header: 900 x 500
Article Preview Thumbnail: 400 x 400 (displays at 200 x 200)
Article Inline Image: 400 wide x any height

Weibo

Cover Image: 920 x 300
Profile Picture: 200 x 200 (displays at 100 x 100)
Banner: 560 x 260
Instream: 120 x 120
Contest Preview: 640 x 640

Appendix C: LINKS

Link Checker

For Chrome: https://chrome.google.com/webstore/detail/check-my-links/ojkcdipcgfaekbe-aelaapakgnjflfglf?hl=en-GB (I know this is out of alpha order, but a good link deserves top billing, don't you think? ;)

Article Marketing Sites

http://goarticles.com/

http://internationalpractice.com/business/

http://thephantomwriters.com/index.php

http://www.articledashboard.com/

http://www.articlegarden.com/

http://www.articlesbase.com/

http://www.articleson.com/

http://www.sitepronews.com/

http://www.selfgrowth.com

http://marniemarcus.com/unplugged/facebook-ad-management/

http://www.isnare.com

http://www.ladypens.com/

http://www.promotionworld.com

http://wahm–articles.com

http://www.writeandpublishyourbook.com/magazine/

https://contributor.yahoo.com/signup.shtml

http://www.ezinearticles.com

Auto Responder Services

AWeber: www.aweber.com/

Constant Contact: www.constantcontact.com/

Robly: https://app.robly.com/invite?rc=f56a53fb2ad6910f3e83ebda

Your Mailing List Provider: www.yourmailinglistprovider.com/

Books and Movies

Complete Library of Entrepreneurial Wisdom: http://www.CLEWbook.com

Presentational Skills for the Next Generation: http://www.amazon.com/dp/B005EA01QO

#Next Level Manners: Business Etiquette for Millennials by Rachel Isgar Ph.D.: http://a. co/cew7qB4

Greeting Card Companies

123Greetings: http://www.123greetings.com

American Greetings: http://www.americangreetings.com/

Blue Mountain: www.bluemountain.com/

Cyberkisses: http://www.cyberkisses.com/

Day Springs: www.dayspring.com/ecards/

Evite: www.evite.com

Hallmark: http://www.hallmark.com/

Jacquie Lawson: www.jacquielawson.com/

Just Wink: https://www.justwink.com/

Operation Write Home: http://operationwritehome.org/

Punchbowl Greetings: http://www.punchbowl.com/invitations/preview/5400a4b424e4b36a 3e000029/5400a56bbf947f655a000111

Send Out Cards: www.sendoutcards.com/

Podcast Directories

Corante-Podcasting: http://podcasting.corante.com/—Weblog with news and events related to podcasting.

Hipcast: http://www.hipcaStcom/—Audio and video podcasting service. Includes news and on-line tour.

iTunes: http://blog.lextext.com/blog/_archives/2005/1/4/225172.html—The iTunes Store puts thousands of free podcasts at your fingertips.

Lextext.com: How to Podcast RIAA Music Under License—http://blog.lextext.com/ blog/_archives/2005/1/4/225172.html—Discussion of legal ways to podcast music. [Podcast is 5.3 MB in size]

The Liberated Syndication Network: http://www.libsyn.com/—Full featured service tailored specifically for media Self-publishing and podcasting. Price is based on usage, changing monthly if needed.

NPR: http://www.npr.org/rss/podcast/podcast_directory.php—Over 50 public radio stations and producers are working with NPR to bring you podcasting.

The Podcast Directory: http://www.podcastdirectory.com/—Up to date and relevant podcast directory.

Podcasting News: http://www.podcastingnews.com/—Information relating to podcasting, a podcast directory, and a user forum.

SkypeCasters: http://www.henshall.com/blog/archives/001056.html—Introducing instructions for SkypeCasting, the solution for podcasters to create audio recordings from interviews and conference calls using Skype.

Skype Forums: http://forum.skype.com/viewtopic.php?t=12788—Recording a Skype Conversation–Discussion thread covering software, techniques, and legal tidbits.

Wikipedia: Podcast –http://en.wikipedia.org/wiki/Podcast—Encyclopedia entry covering basics of the topic.

Promotional Product Supply Companies

4imprint: https://www.4imprint.com/ —offers free samples

Build A Sign: http://www.buildasign.com/

CafePress: www.cafepress.com/

Crown Awards: https://www.crownawards.com/

iPrint: http://www.iprint.com

Judie Glenn Inc: www.judieglenninc.com—ask for Tracey Arehart

Northwest Territorial Mint: http://custom.nwtmint.com/

Overnight Prints: http://www.overnightprints.com/

PC/Nametag®: http://www.pcnametag.com/

Promotional Products: www.promotionalproducts.org/—Get free quotes from multiple vendors

Staples: www.StaplesPromotionalProducts.com

VistaPrint: www.Vistaprint.com

World Class Medals: http://www.worldclassmedals.com/

Zazzle: http://www.zazzle.com/custom/buttons

Quote Sources

Bartleby: http://www.bartleby.com/

Brainy Quote: http://www.brainyquote.com/quotes/keywords/resources.html

Leadership Now: http://www.leadershipnow.com/quotes.html

Quote Garden: http://www.quotegarden.com/index.html

Quoteland: http://www.quoteland.com/

The Quotations Page: http://www.quotationspage.com/

Think Exit: http://thinkexist.com/quotes/american_proverb/

Woopidoo!: http://www.woopidoo.com/

Singing Telegram Services

Aarons Singing Telegrams: http://www.SingingTelegramsLosAngeles.com

American Singing Telegrams: http://www.americansingingtelegrams.com/

Gig Masters Singing Telegrams: http://www.gigmasters.com/SingingTelegram/Singing-Telegram.htm

Happy Entertainment Party Productions: http://www.happyentertainment.com/

The International Singing Telegram Company: http://balloonstunesworldwide.com/

Orange Peel Moses: http://www.customsingingtelegrams.com/

PreppyGrams Singing Telegrams: http://www.preppygrams.com/specialdelivery.html

Sunshine Singing Telegram Service: http://www.sunshinesingingtelegrams.com

The International Singing Telegram Company Inc.: https://www.facebook.com/pages/The-International-Singing-Telegram-Company-Inc/173670102142

Wacky Jack's Singing Telegrams and Balloons: http://www.wackyjacktelegrams.com/

Stock Photos

Tiny Eye: http://www.tineye.com—Reverse image search

Alamy: http://www.alamy.com

Beinecke: http://beinecke.library.yale.edu/digitallibrary

Maps Download MrSid: http://memory.loc.gov/ammem/help/download_sid.html

Big Stock Photo: http://www.bigstockphoto.com

Bing: http://www.bing.com

Can Stock Photo: http://www.canstockphoto.com

CreStock: http://www.crestock.com

DepositPhotos: http://depositphotos.com

Digital Scriptorium: http://bancroft.berkeley.edu/digitalscriptorium—public domain

Dreamstime: https://www.dreamstime.com

EJ Photo: http://www.ejphoto.com—Nature photography

Flickr: https://www.flickr.com—Advanced Search (only search on commercial content etc.)

Fotolia: http://www.foltolia.com

Foto Search: http://www.fotosearch.com

Free Digital Photos: http://www.freedigitalphotos.net

Free Photo: http://www.freefoto.com/index.jsp

Getty: http://www.gettyimages.com/

Google: http://www.images.google.com—Use Advanced Search for Usage Rights, labeled with commercial w/modifications

Icon Finder: http://www.iconfinder.com/illustrations

iStockPhoto: http://www.iStockPhoto.com

Jupiter: http://www.jupiterimages.com

Library of Congress: http://www.loc.gov/index.html— American Memory and Prints and Photographs sections

Morguefile: http://morguefile.com

PhotoSpin: https://www.photospin.com/Default.asp?

Pixabay: http://pixabay.com/

Pixadus: http://pixdaus.com

RGB Stock: www.rgbstock.com—more than 95,000 high quality free stock photos, graphics for illustrations, wallpapers, and backgrounds

Scriptorium: http://www.scriptorium.columbia.edu/public domain

Shutterstock: http://www.shutterstock.com

Stockxchg (FreeImages): http://www.sxc.hu/

ThinkStock Photos: http://www.thinkstockphotos.com/

Top Left Pixel: http://wvs.topleftpixel.com

Visipix: http://www.visipix.com—lots of Japanese art

Visual Photos: http://www.visualphotos.com

Watercolor Textures: https://lostandtaken.com/downloads/category/paint/watercolor-texture/

WebStockPro: http://www.webstockpro.com/

Wikimedia Commons: http://commons.wikimedia.org/wiki/Main_Page—Check images via languages

Wikipedia Public Domain List: http://en.wikipedia.org/wiki/Wikipedia:Public_domain_image_resources/ public domain

You Work for Them: http://www.youworkforthem.com

Teleconference Companies

What is: www.business.com/directory/telecommunications/business_solutions/conferencing/

Buyer's Guide: www.buyerzone.com/telecom_services/telecon_services/buyers_guide5.html

Free Conference: www.freeconference.com/

Teleconference Live: http://teleconference.liveoffice.com

Teleconferencing Services: www.teleconferencingservices.net/

Wholesale Conference Call: www.wholesaleconferencecall.com/

Yugma Desktop Sharing Software: http://vur.me/gmarks/Yugma/

Virtual Assistant Companies

A Clayton's Secretary (Kathie M Thomas): http://vadirectory.net/

Collins Administrative Services (Tracy Collins): http://www.collins–admin.com

MJ Stern, VA: http://www.mjstern–va.com/—Specializes in internet marketing

Streamline Your Marketing (Crystal Pina): http://www.streamlineyourmarketing.com

Virtual Freedom 4 You (Corrie Petersen): http://virtualfreedom4you.com/

Webinar Services

Adobe Acrobat Connect Pro: http://tryit.adobe.com/us/connectpro/universalvoice/?sdid=DNOSU

BrainShark: http://brainshark.com/

Cisco WebEx: http://webex.com/

ClickWebinar: http://www.clickwebinar.com/

DimDim: http://www.dimdim.com/

Elluminate: http://www.elluminate.com/Products/?id=3

Facebook Live: https://live.fb.com/

Freebinar: http://www.freebinar.com/

Free Conference Calling: http://www.freeconferencecalling.com/

Fuze: http://www.fuzemeeting.com/

GatherPlace: http://www.gatherplace.net/start/

Google+ Hangouts: https://plus.google.com/hangouts

GoToMeeting: https://www.gotomeeting.com/

GoToWebinar: http://www.gotomeeting.com/fec/webinar

IBM Lotus Unyte: https://www.unyte.net/

iLinc: http://www.ilinc.com/

Infinite Conference: http://www.infiniteconference.com/

InstantPresenter: http://www.instantpresenter.com/

Intercall: http://www.intercall.com/smb/

Mega Meeting: http://www.megameeting.com/professional.html

Microsoft Office Live Meeting: http://www.microsoft.com/on-line/officE-livE-meet-ing/buy.mspx

Nefsis: http://www.nefsis.com/

Peter Pan Birthday Club: http://www.sjbhealth.org/body_foundation.cfm?id=1875

ReadyTalk: http://www.readytalk.com/

Saba Centra: http://saba.com/

StageToWeb: http://www.stagetoweb.com/livE-event–webcasting.html

Tokbox: http://tokbox.com/

Video Seminar Live: http://www.videoseminarlive.com/

Wix: http://www.wix.com/

Yugma: https://www.yugma.com/

Zoho: http://www.zoho.com/meeting/

Zoom: https://www.zoom.us

Appendix D: RESOURCES

A Grand Life (Play-Doh Fun Facts): https://agrandelife.
net/10-fun-facts-celebrate-world-play-doh-day/

Apron Memories (Tie One On Day): http://www.apronmemories.com/tie-one-on-day/

Born Free USA Pangolin Poster: http://www.bornfreeusa.org/a9f_pangolins.php

Candid Camera 'Best of Highlights' Video: https://youtu.be/-CpzNGhfVio

Clap 4 Health: https://clap4health.com/

Countdown Timer: https://countingdownto.com/

For Pete's Sake Origins: https://www.usatoday.com/story/opinion/2013/02/21/
neuharth-for-petes-sake-how-did-it-start/1937089/

Greeting Card Universe (For Pete's Sake card): https://www.greetingcarduniverse.
com/holidays/nationalandinternationaldays/forpetessakedayfebruary26/
grumpy-pete-february-26th-for-1419282

How Stuff Works (progressive dinner party): https://recipes.howstuffworks.com/menus/how-
to-throw-a-progressive-dinner-party.htm

National Bison Association: https://bisoncentral.com/

National Grange Association: https://www.nationalgrange.org/

National Memory Day Poetry Collection: https://www.poetryarchive.org/content/
national-memory-day-collection

National Moth Week Website: http://nationalmothweek.org/

National Punctuation Day Website: http://www.nationalpunctuationday.com/celebrate.html

National Wildlife Federation (Bison petition): https://online.nwf.org/site/
Advocacy?cmd=display&page=UserAction&id=2456

Puzzles USA Today: http://puzzles.usatoday.com/

Quizland: http://quizland.com/cotd.htm

Sales & Marketing (SMM): https://salesandmarketing.com/

Uncommon Goods (gardening gifts): https://www.uncommongoods.com

YouTube LULU Day Video: https://www.youtube.com/watch?v=WTE82HI5iOU

#Next Level Manners: Business Etiquette for Millennials by Rachel Isgar Ph.D.: http://a.
co/cew7qB4

About the Author

Having been a business owner for most of her adult life, operating a multi–million-dollar surgical clinic and a local barbecue take-out to list just a couple, have given Ginger Marks the insight needed to assist business owners from all walks of life.

Ginger is the owner of the Calomar, LLC which holds her DocUmeant family of companies. The various entities all work towards a common goal that just happens to be their tagline; "We Make YOU Look GOOD!" Her services include both publishing and digital design assistance. She is proud of the fact that she is able to give high quality, efficient service at a remarkably reasonable rate. It is for this reason she chose to list her publishing company in New York City while residing in Florida.

When Ginger decided to embark on a writing career it was of no surprise to her mother, who herself is a published author. Her love for the arts is what spurred her to hone her talents as a digital designer, offering services to business owners and authors alike.

DocUmeant.net offers editing and writing services; DocUmeantDesigns.com, as you would guess, focuses on designs ranging from websites to book covers and layouts to buttons and business stationary needs; while DocUmeantPublishing.com's focus was begun with the self-published author in mind. Now with ten years of experience in publishing she has built her success in the global community.

Ginger is a member of DesignFirms where she is a top-rated designer, SPANpro (Small Publishers Association of North America), IBPA (International Book Publishers Association), DBW (Digital Book World), and is on the board of FAPA as VP Communications (Florida Authors and Publishers Association).

Most recently, Ginger was awarded for her generous contribution to internet business while helping others achieve their goals in publishing and marketing. The Golden Mouse Award was presented to her by Women In e-Commerce on Oct 28, 2016. In 2012 she was awarded VIP membership to Covington's Who's Who and her publishing company, DocUmeant Publishing, was awarded the 2012 and 2016 New York Award in the Publishing Consultants and Services category by the U.S. Commerce Association (USCA). She is the recipient of the 2015, 16, and 17 Clearwater, FL Design Firm Award and has won book cover design awards and is a multiple award winner for her Weird & Wacky Holiday Marketing Guide from FAPA.

In her spare time, she loves to do crafts of all sorts and sing. And yes, she is a little wacky at times too which keeps her fun and inspiring. Ginger lives in Florida where she works side-by-side with her husband, Philip, who is VP Editing for DocUmeant Publishing.

To contact Ginger whether for publish, design, or interviews you may reach her at ginger.marks@documeantdesigns.com or at 727-565-2130.

Additional Works by Ginger Marks

Visit Ginger's Amazon Author Central for more information or to purchase her books.
https://www.amazon.com/Ginger-Marks/e/B005ECOWD0/

The companion Playbook for the Annual *Weird & Wacky Holiday Marketing Guide* l will assist you in planning and tracking your holiday marketing success using the tools, tips, and resources found in the *Weird & Wacky Holiday Marketing Guide*.

- Easily plan and track your marketing
- Organized by month
- Room to write notes
- Track your success
- No expiration date! Start using any time.

Print: $12.97
Available at Amazon.com

ISBN-13:
978-1937801779

Much has changed over the years in the public speaking arena. We have so many new and challenging tools at our disposal that we are no longer consigned to countless hours to travel from city to city to share our knowledge.

The Internet has opened the doors to people from all places and races. At the click of a button, you can share your information in many forms of multi-media. With the availability of hosting online conferences and collaborations in both text-only and A/V environments, as are offered by Skype Conference™, Hot Conference™ and desktop sharing applications such as Yugma™, as well as teleconferences, the modes and means are so plentiful that more and more savvy business owners are venturing into the public speaking arena. It is a well thought out, concise, instructional manual written in a manner that all can comprehend. Within the contents of this guide, you will learn the skills necessary to enable you to present your information in such a way that you will capture the attention and hearts of your eager audience.

Available in Print $14.95
Also available in Digital $9.95

Print ISBN:
978-0-9788831-4-0
Digital ISBN:
978-0-9832122-7-0

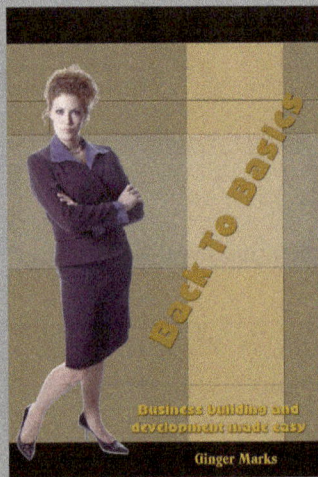

Back to Basics is a collection of articles designed to assist the new business owner to jump start their business or the seasoned profession to put the punch back into their chosen career. It begins with a two part series on the Nuts and Bolts of Business Building and continues from there to the ever important Marketing Basics. As marketing is an issue for each and every business owner no matter their business or circumstances this section is presented in three parts. This eBook comes in Kindle & PDF versions and at $2.99 it is a real bargain.

$2.99

Kindle Edition

Download: https://www.amazon.com/ Back-Basics-Ginger-Marks-ebook/dp/B00A8SJ2D0

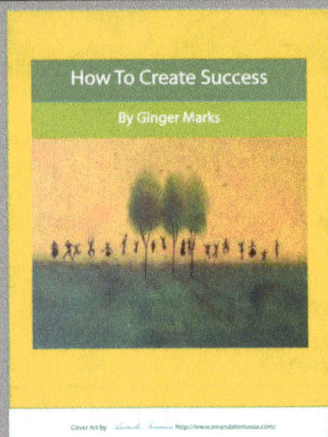

How To Create Success is the first eBook offering. Its bold colorful cover image entitled Jumping for Joy was designed by Amanda Tomasoa of Art by Amanda. The seven chapters contained within combine seven of the most highly rated articles written by Ginger at the time of publishing. One article "Contagious Influence" is currently the number one requested article and has been published in a magazine for writers titled 'Newbie News'. This is a free ebook and available for immediate download.

FREE Download: http://www.gingermarksbooks.com/PDFs/ HowToCreateSuccess.pdf

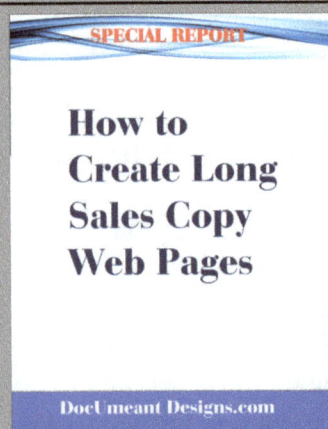

In this report you will learn how to create and effective *Long Sales Copy Web Page* and why you might need one. As you read through this report if you come to the conclusion that a *Long Sales Copy Web Page* is the right tool for your business, I highly recommend you use the company or individual with the working knowledge and integrity to create the site you need to get your important message across to your target market.

If you haven't a clue how to decipher who your target market is then that it the best place to start. Without this knowledge no matter how compelling you product or service message is, it will result in an ineffective campaign. This will end up costing you valuable time and money. Although this is beyond the context of this Special Report there are a myriad of resources available to you today online to help you along the way. As well, there are coaches who specialize in this area of expertise. Feel free to contact me and I will be happy to point you in the right direction.

To receive this FREE REPORT sign up for her monthly *Words of Wisdom eZine* here: http://www.gingermarksbooks.com/

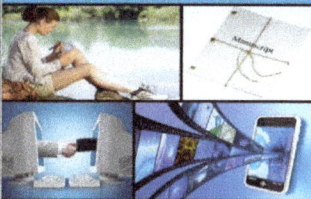

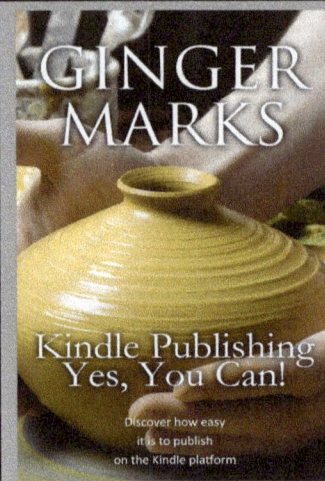

WEIRD & WACKY HOLIDAY MARKETING GUIDE
COMPLETE YOUR COLLECTION TODAY!

Previous Editions Available here:
http://holidaymarketingguide.com/past.html

Affiliate Marketing Opportunities available at
http://www.HolidayMarketingGuide.com!

* 9 7 8 1 9 3 7 8 0 1 8 7 8 *